HARVARD DIVIDED

by Linda Ayres

An exhibition held at the Fogg Art Museum,
Harvard University, Cambridge, Massachusetts
June 3 through October 10, 1976

ON THE COVER: *College Buildings*, 1798, by John Abbot (1777-1854). Lent by Harvard University Archives. Cat. no. 55. Photograph by Michael Nedzweski

LIBRARY OF CONGRESS CATALOGING IN PUBLICATION DATA

Ayres, Linda, 1947-
   Harvard divided.

Bibliography: p. 168
   Includes index.
   1. Harvard University—History—Revolution, 1775-1783—Exhibitions. 2. American loyalists—Massachusetts—Cambridge—Exhibitions. 3. Cambridge, Mass.—Exhibitions. 4. United States—History—Revolution, 1775-1783—Portraits—Exhibitions. I. Harvard University. William Hayes Fogg Art Museum. II. Title.
E270.H37A94   974.4'4   76-10787
ISBN 0-916724-05-0

This exhibition and catalogue were organized with the aid of a grant from the National Endowment for the Arts in Washington, D.C., a Federal agency.

Typesetting by Dumar Typesetting, Inc.
Printing by the Meriden Gravure Company
Design by Lance Hidy
Printed in the United States of America

Acknowledgments

The idea for *Harvard Divided* originated with Bernard Bailyn, a leading scholar of the American Revolution. Christopher Jedrey, who is writing his dissertation under the direction of Professor Bailyn, helped to develop some of the themes. He suggested Peter Oliver's "portrait gallery" as one focus of the exhibition, proposed the Quincys as the example of a family torn by the Revolution, and wrote the essay on the Hollis family. Additional research assistance came from Bonnie Yochelson who worked diligently to provide a wealth of important information. David Brewster read through the manuscript and suggested many constructive changes. And Louise Ambler taught me a great deal about exhibitions and catalogues. To these people I owe my deepest gratitude.

William Bond shared his knowledge of the Hollises, and David Mitten helped interpret the symbols connected with that family of Harvard benefactors. Andrew Oliver and Edmund Quincy were extremely generous with information about their illustrious families. Many kind individuals in both Canada and England responded to my queries about Loyalists who fled Massachusetts, and the *Telegraph Journal*, St. John, New Brunswick, helped by publicizing my search for Tory portraits. I am grateful to Norman Hirschl, Stuart Feld, and Jane Richards of Hirschl & Adler Galleries who also assisted in the portrait search, as well as to R. Peter Mooz and Barbara N. Parker for invaluable advice on portrait attributions. Kathryn Buhler suggested sources for information on silver, and David Wheatland and Ebenezer Gay lent their expertise in scientific instruments.

I would like to thank also the many individuals at the facilities I visited who took time from their busy schedules to assist me: Winifred Collins, Massachusetts Historical Society; Veronica Cunningham, Map Room, Pusey Library; Mona Dearborn, Catalog of American Portraits, National Portrait Gallery, Smithsonian Institution; Leo Flaherty, Massachusetts Archives; Cynthia Fleming, New England Historic Genealogical Society; Lucretia Giese, Laura Luckey, Sandra Emerson, Wendy Cooper, and Stephanie Loeb Stepanek, Museum of Fine Arts, Boston; John V. Harvey and Ruth Lynch, Middlesex County Courthouse; Harley Holden and Karen Lewis, Harvard University Archives; Jack Jackson, Boston Athenaeum; Carolyn Jakeman, Marte Shaw, and Eleanor Garvey, Houghton Library; and Frank Lawton, Boston Public Library.

Other kind people took time to answer my numerous inquiries. Morton Bradley, Jo Brewer, Douglas Bryant, Georgia Bumgardner, Harriet Ropes Cabot, Mrs. Hall Carpenter, Giovanni Castano, Charles D. Childs, John

Coolidge, Wendell Garrett, Wendell S. Hadlock, Zoltan Haraszti, Richard B. Harrington and Mrs. John Nicholas Brown, H. Hobart Holly, Henry Lee, Robert Lovet, Agnes Mongan, Sandy Morgan, Carolyn Owens, Jane Pike, Isabel Stuebe, Dorothy Vaughan, Cornelius C. Vermeule, S. Morton Vose II, and Walter Muir Whitehill were all of invaluable assistance.

Substantial financial support for *Harvard Divided* — and indeed, for all three bicentennial exhibitions — came from the National Endowment for the Arts. I am also indebted to Charles W. Eliot II and the Council of the Cambridge Historical Society for enabling us to conserve the Vassall portraits.

All of the Fogg's departments have aided in the creation of this exhibition. To them I extend warm thanks. I am indebted to Lance Hidy for both the design of the catalogue, and for supervising the many details of its production.

I am especially grateful to the lenders who agreed to part with their treasured possessions for such a long time. Without them, the exhibition would have been impossible. And special thanks go to our Bicentennial Advisory Committee who stood ready to assist all three of the Museum's bicentennial projects in every way. The members of this committee are: Thomas Boylston Adams; Louise Todd Ambler; Bernard Bailyn; William H. Bond; Charles D. Childs; John P. Coolidge; I. Bernard Cohen; Donald Fleming; David McCord; Agnes Mongan; William Pinkerton; Giles Whitcomb; and Walter Muir Whitehill.

Linda Ayres

Contents

Illustrations

List of Lenders

American Antiquarian Society
Anonymous Lenders
Apthorp House
Boston Public Library
Cambridge Historical Society
Christ Church, Cambridge
Collection of Historical Scientific Instruments, Harvard University
Congregational Library, Boston
Dietrich Brothers Americana Corporation
Ebenezer Gay
Harvard College Library
Harvard University Archives
Harvard University Portrait Collection
Houghton Library
Library of Congress
Massachusetts Historical Society
Frederick Strong Moseley III
Museum of Fine Arts, Boston
Newburyport Public Library
The Oliver Family
Edmund Quincy
Williams College Museum of Art
Yale University Art Gallery

Foreword

Harvard Divided is the last of three exhibitions mounted at the Fogg Art Museum in commemoration of the nation's Bicentennial. The first and second, devoted to Benjamin Franklin and Lafayette respectively, concentrated on the many ways the intellectual concerns and devotion to the revolutionary cause of these popular heroes of two continents were linked to the life of the College.

Harvard Divided treats a subject which has generally been overshadowed by the more dramatic events of the Revolution. It concerns the personal tragedies of a civil war and the pull of loyalties that divided the friendships and, sometimes, the families of Harvard graduates. For, as Bernard Bailyn has pointed out, "the opponents of the Revolution — the administration itself — were as convinced as were the leaders of the Revolutionary movement that they were themselves the victims of conspiratorial designs" (*The Ideological Origins of the American Revolution,* p. 150).

The predicament of these victims is further illuminated as the exhibition illustrates the way in which the Harvard and Cambridge communities were affected by the Revolution. The physical and administrative changes brought about by the war are recalled by a collection of maps, topographical views, and documents. The portraits confront us with the likenesses of the many individuals whose fates were determined by both their own choices and the momentum of the events by which they were overtaken.

The exhibition is the result of collaboration between Harvard's Department of History and the Fogg Museum. Bernard Bailyn, Winthrop Professor of History, originated the idea for the show, gave valuable counsel and support, and provided the catalogue with a penetrating introduction. Linda Ayres, assistant to the director at the Fogg, gave form to Professor Bailyn's ideas. She has been responsible for the enterprise from the initial stages of study, research, and seeking of material, to mounting the exhibition and writing the catalogue. The Fogg is deeply beholden to both colleagues.

We should also like to acknowledge our debt to the National Endowment for the Arts for a grant that helped organize the exhibition and catalogue.

S. S.

Introduction

The American Revolution was no unanimous upsurge of patriotic fervor. Like all great public upheavals it erupted only after years of growing discontent, failing efforts at compromise, and bitter controversy. Opinions of men of good will on both sides of the issues differed increasingly as the breach between Britain and America widened. Close friends separated and fought on opposite sides; families divided. We do not know precisely how many Americans remained loyal to Britain. Many disguised their feelings and remained inactive during the war years. But we do know that between fifty thousand and eighty thousand Americans left the thirteen colonies as loyalist refugees, and though many later returned and others managed to retain property and friendly ties in their old communities, there was a significant disruption of American society as a consequence.

The incidence of loyalism varied from region to region. The highest concentration was in the middle states, New York particularly, where the British army gave protection until 1783. New England and Virginia had relatively few loyalists, but even there loyalism was an important fact, and its significance is vividly illustrated in this exhibition.

For while New England as a whole was overwhelmingly favorable to the Revolutionary movement and provided much of its initial impetus and leadership, the Boston area, particularly Cambridge and the Harvard College community, was sharply divided. Cambridge, with its wealthy Tory merchants established in some of the finest houses of provincial America, and the alumni body of the College, with its many officials, lawyers, and landowning gentry, contained an important group of opponents of the Revolution. They were neither unusually self-serving nor particularly backward nor singularly stupid. Their opposition, while lacking in imagination, perhaps, and insensitive to the Patriots' higher aspirations, was conceived in terms of perfectly reasonable arguments and nourished by an understandable if conservative desire to maintain an established existence. Since they were the losers, history has swept them aside; but they were important elements in the Revolutionary situation. Their views, their way of life, and their fortunes must be understood. "Harvard Divided," an exhibition of local materials that are of national importance, is an effort to portray in graphic form the two faces of the Revolution as it can now, after two hundred years, be properly understood.

The exhibition contains five distinct focuses. It presents the Revolution first from the point of view of one of the most flamboyant and uncompromising loyalists, the exiled Chief Justice, Peter Oliver. Using as a narrative thread Oliver's vitriolic, at times uproarious, history of events in Massachusetts, *The Origins & Progress of The American Rebellion,* the exhibition shows in a remarkable collection of matched verbal and visual portraits the major antagonists of the struggle that took place in Boston and Cambridge two hundred years ago. Through the generosity of the Oliver and Quincy families, and through the kindness of many other individuals and institutions with local connections, almost the entire leadership on both sides is displayed in portraiture.

The exhibition of the division at the heart of the Revolution continues in a second form, that of Harvard College. The struggles of its alumni over the Revolutionary issues are traced through the efforts of Jonathan Mayhew to defeat a suspected attempt to impose an Episcopal hierarchy on the American colonies; then through the activities and divisions of the Quincy family; and finally through the decisive and most sensational episode in the long controversy between the interrelated Hutchinson-Oliver clan and the Adamses and other Patriot leaders.

The third and fourth groupings of materials are more purely graphic. They display the appearance of Harvard and the town of Cambridge in the era of the Revolution. A fine group of college and town views, some of them never displayed before, gives a vivid impression of the still rural ambience in which the early episodes of the Revolution took place. These impressions are made still more vivid by the physical survival of the Loyalists' mansions, which are shown in modern photographs as well as in contemporary sketches.

The exhibition closes with a display of the remarkable history of the Hollis family's gifts to Harvard in the 18th century. The Hollises were wealthy English nonconformists, mainly Baptists, who saw in Harvard College the means of disseminating throughout the world their intense commitment to religious freedom and political liberty. Not merely donors to the financial welfare of the College but ideologues and propagandists, they sent over from England in the course of the eighteenth century funds for buildings, endowments for professorships, and above all a sizeable library of the writings of British libertarians. All of this was part of the effort the family sustained for three generations to assist Harvard in what they took to be its main task, the furtherance of the cause of liberty. Their benefactions, particularly the "library of liberty" they donated, undoubtedly heightened the College's sensitivity to the Patriotic side of the central issues of the Revolution.

This exhibition, displaying materials of both Patriots and Loyalists, responds to the challenge that the Revolution now poses to the historical imagination: to understand the reason and humanity on both sides — while appreciating fully the liberating spirit of the Revolution and its achievements, to see at the same time the sense and sensibility of those who were defeated.

Bernard Bailyn
Winthrop Professor of History

I. Peter Oliver's Portrait Gallery

In 1781, while exiled in England, Peter Oliver completed a manuscript giving his interpretation of the Revolution.[1] Peter Oliver was the last chief justice of the Massachusetts Superior Court under the crown. His relatives and friends also held important offices in the Bay Province. It is not difficult to understand, therefore, why *The Origins & Progress of the American Rebellion* chronicled the collapse of Oliver's aristocratic world in bitter terms.

Judge Oliver could not understand what he termed this "unnatural rebellion." The American colonies, he believed, had been overindulged, pampered, and ruled with benevolence by their mother country. He blamed the rebellion on the greed and ambition of a few rabble-rousers who effectively used propaganda to goad the people into overthrowing British rule.

The author confined his history to Massachusetts, "as it was this Province where I resided, & was most intimate to the Transactions of; & as it was the *Volcano* from whence issued all the Smoak, Flame & Lava which hath since enveloped the whole British american Continent, for the length of above 1700 miles."[2] He informed his readers that he would relate the facts, the characters, and the consequences of the "Progress of the Dæmon.... In short you will see every Thing, sacred & profane, twisted into all Shapes to serve the Purposes of Rebellion; & Earth & Hell ransacked for Tools to work the Fabrick with."[3]

As the first major event on the road to rebellion, Oliver cited the feud between two leading Massachusetts families—the Hutchinsons and the Otises—that began when Thomas Hutchinson, instead of James Otis, Sr., was appointed chief justice in 1760. James Otis, Jr., Oliver wrote, swore revenge on the Hutchinson faction and promised to set the Province "in a Flame." He founded the rebel movement with the aid of such men as Sam Adams, John

Hancock, and members of the dissenting clergy or "Black Regiment": Charles Chauncy, Jonathan Mayhew, and Samuel Cooper.

Oliver sketched the characters of these incendiaries who, he said, had let passion override reason (see cat. nos. 2-8), and afterwards told the reader: "I have done Sir! for the present, with my Portraits. If you like them, & think them ornamental for your Parlour, pray hang them up in it; for I assure you, that most of them justly demerit a *Suspension*."[4]

He admitted that most of the shades of his portraits were very dark, but explained: "My business was to draw true Portraits. If Nature hath been distorted by the wild Freaks of the various human Passions, neither she or I ought to be blamed."[5]

Oliver's lengthy portrait of Thomas Hutchinson (cat. no. 30), in stark contrast to those of the Patriots, was effusive in its praise. An excerpt will indicate the high regard in which he held his friend and relative:

> In private Life, Mr. *Hutchinson* was the Scholar, without Pedantry — the polite Gentleman, without Affectation — the social Companion, without Reservedness — affable, without the last Tincture of Pride — in Commerce, undisguised & open — in Morals, regular without Severity — in Expression of his Sentiments, candid & void of Guile — liberal in his Charity, without Ostentation of Partiality — amiable in Domestick Life, distinguished by conjugal Fidelity & attention, parental Attention, & an humane, tender & condescending Behavior to his dependant Domesticks — his Religion sat gracefull on his conduct; it was manly & free, undebased by Hypocrisy, Enthusiasm, or Superstition; it embraced all Mankind.[6]

According to Oliver's account, an event that ranked second only to the Hutchinson-Otis conflict as a cause of the Revolution was the Stamp Act of 1765, passed to recompense the British for the money they spent to protect (as Oliver saw it) the colonists from the French in Canada. This act gave "Stimulus to the Passions & Designs of the Factious," and raised the "Hydra of Rebellion." Its repeal, in 1766, convinced Otis and his "myrmidons" of their power and, from that point on, they could not be stopped.

They next defied the Townshend Acts — the 1767 duties on tea, glass, paper, and other articles — with smuggling and non-importation agreements. The colonists cut back their use of elaborate imported clothing and other taxable items, and began manufacturing their own. The women spun cloth six days a week, "& on the seventh, the Parsons took their Turns and spun out their Prayers & Sermons to a long Thread of Politicks. . . ."[7]

By 1768, Governor Bernard, who had arrived in 1760, was losing control of the government, and two regiments of British troops were ordered from Halifax. In 1769, according to

Oliver, the colonists succeeded in having Bernard removed from office. Now mob rule prevailed. The Boston Massacre and the Tea Party brought the Revolution closer. After these incidents, the rebels "found they had past the *Rubicon*; it was now, Neck or Nothing."[8]

In 1774, Thomas Hutchinson, who had replaced Bernard as governor, was himself replaced by Gen. Thomas Gage, who arrived with four regiments of troops. Boston was an armed camp. Britain's prime minister, Lord North, had closed the port of Boston as punishment for the destruction of the tea. While Gage was attempting to rule with the help of Tory mandamus councillors, the rebels were establishing their own provincial governments. Soon thereafter, in 1775, the battles of Lexington and Concord commenced the bloody war.

Peter Oliver and the other Loyalists were forced to flee and to spend the remainder of their lives in exile in Canada and England. They lost their homes, businesses, high political offices, possessions, and sometimes, their families. Oliver saw America, which was once "flowing with Milk & Honey," turned into what he considered a living hell. "And all these Distresses they have been plunged into, by an *Otis*, an *Adams,* a *Franklin,* & a few others of the most abandoned Characters, aided by a Set of Priests, who are a disgrace to Christianity."[9]

Oliver's portraits, though extremely partisan, are still those of an intelligent participant in those events which we seek to understand. Moreover, they add another perspective to our usual interpretation of the Revolution. So look for a moment at Peter Oliver, late chief justice of Massachusetts, and then, through his eyes, at Harvard's rebellious sons.

---

1. This history was not published until 1961.
2. Douglass Adair and John A. Schutz, eds., *Peter Oliver's Origins and Progress of the American Rebellion,* p. 9.
3. *Ibid.,* p. 26.
4. *Ibid.,* p. 45.
5. *Ibid.,* p. 144.
6. *Ibid.,* p. 34.
7. *Ibid.,* p. 64.
8. *Ibid.,* p. 103.
9. *Ibid.,* p. 149.

1. WILLIAMS, William (1727-1791), English

Peter Oliver (1713-1791), 1781

Oil on panel. H. 29.3 x 40 cm. Signed and dated, bottom of tomb-
stone: W Williams P / 1781
Provenance: Rev. John R. Hutchinson, great-grandson of the subject;
  Mrs. John R. Hutchinson, his widow; Mrs. F. E. Oliver, Boston;
  Miss Susan L. Oliver, her daughter
Lent by the Oliver Family

After several years of working with the Olivers, Hutchinsons, and Clarkes in the shipping trade, Peter Oliver (A.B.
1730) moved thirty miles outside of Boston to Middle-
borough. There he built a manor house, "Oliver Hall," a
successful iron works, and a prosperous farm. In 1744, he
began his public service career when he was appointed
justice of the peace for Plymouth County. Three years
later, he was promoted to the Court of Common Pleas
and, in 1756, to the Superior Court. Also in 1756 he was
elected to serve in the House of Representatives and then
the Council. He was named chief justice of Massachusetts
in 1772.

Oliver incurred the Patriots' ire by endorsing a proposal
to pay colonial judges out of royal revenues. They asked
Thomas Hutchinson to remove him from the bench.
Hutchinson, who had recommended Oliver for the position, and whose daughter, Sarah, had married Peter
Oliver, Jr., refused to do so. The House of Representatives
thereupon began impeachment proceedings against Judge
Oliver for "high crimes and misdemeanors." Although the
impeachment attempt was unsuccessful — Hutchinson refused to preside — the Whigs were determined to make
it as difficult as possible for Oliver to carry out his judicial
duties. When he came to court, juries refused to sit. Mobs
tried to keep his carriage from entering town. It is said
that he narrowly escaped several assassination attempts.
Finally, the pressures became so great that "Sir Peter
Lack-Learning" was forced to promise not to exercise the
powers of his office.

An active member of the royally-appointed Mandamus Council (see cat. no. 10), Peter Oliver remained in Boston when General Gage sealed off the town. But in March 1776, Oliver and his niece, Jenny Clarke, sailed for Nova Scotia with the British troops. A few months later, he arrived in London and wrote in his diary:

> Thanks be to Heaven, I am now in a Place where I can be protected from the Harpy Claws of that Rebellion which is now tearing out its own Bowels, in America, as well as destroying all, who in any Degree oppose its Progress.[1]

Oliver toured England with Thomas Hutchinson, received a D.C.L. degree from Oxford on 4 July 1776, and finally settled in suburban Birmingham in 1778. He was appointed governor of New Ireland (Northern Maine), but the war precluded his return to the colonies.

A novelist, artist, musician, teacher, and adventurer, the Englishman William Williams arrived in Philadelphia in 1747 and established himself there as a portrait painter. He was successful, teaching a young pupil named Benjamin West and building one of the first theatres in that city. By 1780, Williams had returned to England, where he spent his last years as a beggar. He died in an almshouse in Bristol in 1791.

Williams painted this portrait of Oliver after returning to England, where Oliver was living in exile. The painting depicts Oliver mourning for his wife, Mary Clarke (sister of Richard Clarke; see cat. no. 42), who had died in Massachusetts in 1775. The inscription on the tomb reads:

> *Ah Mary holiest of wives never to be forgotten*
> *Great virtue has gone to heaven.*

---

1. *Sibley's Harvard Graduates: Biographical Sketches of Those Who Attended Harvard College*, 8:758. Peter Oliver's diary, 13 June 1776. This document is now in the British Museum.

2. JACKMAN, W. G. (dates unknown), English, after Joseph Blackburn (fl. 1752-1763), English

James Otis, Jr. (1725-1783), after 1841

Steel engraving. Approx. plate mark: H. 20.3 x 13.3 cm.
Inscribed, below image: Engd by W. G. Jackman / J Otis. / N.Y.D. Appleton & Co.
Provenance: Henry F. Sewall
Lent by the Museum of Fine Arts, Boston; Harvey D. Parker Collection (P 12557)

> The first Character . . . which I shall exhibit [wrote Peter Oliver] will be the young Mr. *Otis*, as he was the first who broke down the Barriers of Government to let in the *Hydra* of Rebellion. . . . Mr. *Otis* was designed, by Nature, for a Genius; but it seemed as if, by the Impetuosity of his Passions, he had wrested himself out of her Hands before she had complemented her Work; for his Life seemed to have adopted that Maxim . . . "Better to reign in Hell than serve in Heaven." And his whole Life seemd to be a Comment on his Text. . . . He was devoid of all Principle; & would, as a Lawyer, take Fees on both sides, in which he had been detected in open Court.[1]

Brilliant yet unstable, "Jemmy" Otis (A.B. 1743) came from a politically oriented family, long powerful in Plymouth County. After graduation from Harvard, he studied for a while under the renowned lawyer Jeremiah Gridley (A.B. 1725) and then began practicing law in Plymouth. In 1749, Otis moved to Boston, was appointed justice of the peace, and came to represent the city's merchant interests. He married Ruth Cunningham, the daughter of an affluent merchant, in 1755.[2]

Although his father, James Otis, Sr. — who had been closely allied with former governor William Shirley — had expected the appointment of chief justice in 1760, the position went instead to Thomas Hutchinson. Young Otis accused Hutchinson and his relatives of establishing a family oligarchy.[3] According to Hutchinson, he swore to "set the Province in a Flame."

The two clashed again in 1761 when the controversy arose over the writs of assistance (general search warrants giving customs officers the right to enter homes and shops). Otis resigned from the Admiralty Court to argue (for no fee) against the writs, in one of the first cases over which Hutchinson presided as chief justice, against his old teacher Jeremiah Gridley. In a long and fiery oration, delivered in the Old State House on 24 February 1761, he

called the writs the "worst instrument of arbitrary power, the most destructive to English liberty, and the fundamental principles of the constitution." Arguing that "an Act against the constitution is void," he maintained that the writs were surely a violation of an individual's constitutional rights. He asked the court to "demolish this monster of oppression, and . . . tear into rags this remnant of Starchamber Tyranny."[3] John Adams recorded that every man, including himself, went away from the courtroom prepared to fight the writs of assistance, and "then and there the child Independence was born."[4] Although Otis lost his legal case, the popular response to his argument rendered the writs unenforceable.

This case brought Otis great popularity and, later in 1761, he was elected to the General Court. His popularity prevailed until the years 1764-65, when he appeared to waver in his dedication to the colonial cause. *The Rights of the British Colonies Asserted and Proved,* published during the Sugar Act crisis of 1764, denied Britain's right to tax the colonists without representation in Parliament.[5] But in 1765 he wrote two other pamphlets that reflected a 180-degree shift in his views. Now he argued in favor of Parliament's authority to tax and changed his opinion regarding colonial representation. In his *Brief Remarks in the Defence of the Halifax Libel,* Otis told his countrymen they had been "long overindulged with a more ample subordinate legislation, than the wisdom of administration thinks the good of the whole Empire will admit of their enjoying any longer."[6] Gov. Francis Bernard was pleased with Otis's repentance "in Sackcloth & ashes."

Otis's vacillation cost him popularity and aroused the suspicions of both Patriots and Loyalists. The newspapers attacked him as an "inveterate enemy," a "double-faced Jacobite Whig," and "Jemmy Split." But with the victory of the Patriots in the General Court in 1766, in which the Hutchinson-Oliver clique was ousted, Otis was elected Speaker of the House.

Otis retired from politics, for the most part, after 1769, the year in which he was severely clubbed on the head during a coffee house brawl with customs officers. His injuries, along with the continuing tension from his personal "crisis of loyalty," led to a mental breakdown.[7]

Although Otis had several periods of improved mental health, he was confined to someone's care for the rest of his life. After his father's death, he went to live in Andover, where he destroyed all his books, papers, and letters. On 23 May 1783 he died as he had always hoped he would, struck by a bolt of lightning.

Joseph Blackburn (see cat. no. 37) painted a half-length portrait of Otis in 1755. W. G. Jackman, an Englishman who came to New York in 1841 to work for various publishers, made this engraving after the Blackburn portrait.

1. Adair and Schutz, eds. *Peter Oliver's Origins*, pp. 36-37.
2. His wife was a Tory, as was his sister Mary's husband, John Gray.
3. Ironically, John Adams accused the Otis family of the same offense (see Butterfield, et al., eds., *Diary and Autobiography of John Adams*, 2:20, 66).
4. John J. Waters, Jr., *The Otis Family in Provincial and Revolutionary Massachusetts*, p. 123.
5. Bernard Bailyn, *The Ordeal of Thomas Hutchinson*, p. 56.
6. "Every British subject . . . ," Otis declared, "is by law of God and nature, by the common law, and by Act of Parliament, . . . entitled to all the natural, essential, inherent, and inseparable rights of our fellow subjects in Great Britain" (Ellen Brennan, "James Otis: Recreant and Patriot," p. 697).
7. *Ibid.*, p. 710.
8. Waters, p. 181. His sister, Mercy Otis Warren (cat. no. 9), sketched Otis's psychological state in her play, *The Adulateur* (1772). As Brutus, he is tormented by doubts about which stand to take.

3. Copy after COPLEY, John Singleton (1738-1815), American

Samuel Adams (1722-1803)

Oil on panel. H. 35.5 x 24.1 cm.
Provenance: Thomas Melvill, Esq.; Priscilla Melvill, his daughter
Harvard University Portrait Collection; bequest of Priscilla Melvill, 1863 (H 48)

Peter Oliver stated that an American painter observed that "if he wished to draw a Picture of the Devil, that he would get *Sam Adams* to sit for him. . . ." Oliver continued:

> . . . a very ordinary Physiognomist would, at a transient View of his Countenance, develope the Malignity of his Heart. He was a Person of Understanding, but it was discoverable rather by a Shrewdness than Solidity of Judgment; & he understood human Nature, in low life, so well, that he could turn the Minds of the great Vulgar as well as the small into any Course that he might chuse; perhaps he was a singular Instance in this Kind; & he never failed of employing his Abilities to the vilest Purposes.[1]

The most radical of the Patriots, Adams (A.B. 1740) hated the British so much that he trained his dog Queue to bite Redcoats. So extreme were his views that even some of his colleagues in the American cause distrusted him.

Adams was a failure in business. He was first a maltster, then a tax collector, but basically he relied on his wife's earnings for support, and possibly on gifts from his wealthy friend and protégé, John Hancock.

It was not until 1765 that Sam Adams came forth as a radical leader. An organizer, he led the Sons of Liberty and proposed the Committees of Correspondence to establish an intercolonial movement. A propagandist, he wrote political essays under twenty-five pseudonyms for Boston papers and supplied printers in other cities with a serialized "Journal of Events" which listed British atrocities;

and he was an active force in provoking the Stamp Act riots, the Boston Tea Party, and other popular actions.

Increasingly angry and disaffected by post-war society, he had an erratic political career at the state level, culminated by his election as governor in 1793. When he died in 1803, one gentleman remarked that

> Our friend had lived long enough to see the complete fulfillment of all his labors and wishes, and so long that his usefulness to the public was lost, and he had almost become burthensome to himself; even so long that he wished to depart.[2]

This painting was bequeathed in a will dated 1856 as "a small original portrait of the late Governor Samuel Adams, by Copley." However, it appears to be an early copy after the half-length portrait (owned by the City of Boston) which John Hancock commissioned Copley to paint in 1772. The larger work depicts Adams confronting Thomas Hutchinson on the day after the Boston Massacre. At that time, Adams gave the governor the choice of sending the British troops to Castle William — which course he finally took — or having Boston invaded by the country militia.[3]

A label on the back indicates that this small portrait bust of Sam Adams was painted for his friend, Thomas Melvill (1751-1832; honorary A.M. 1773), grandfather of the author Herman Melville *(Moby Dick)*. Melvill (see cat. no. 39) had just returned from Scotland in 1773 to establish a business in Boston when he joined his fellow Patriots as an "Indian" in the Boston Tea Party.

---

1. Adair and Schutz, eds., *Peter Oliver's Origins, p. 39.*
2. *Sibley's,* 10:464.
3. Fort William on Castle Island in Boston Harbor, usually known as "Castle William," was a garrison of the provincial militia, about three miles off the coast. Royal troops, stationed there after 1770, provided protection for Loyalists who fled for their safety. Castle William was destroyed during the British evacuation of Boston.

4. COPLEY, John Singleton (1738-1815), American

John Hancock (1737-1793), ca. 1770-72

Oil on canvas. H. 75 x 62.2 cm.
Provenance: Henry Lee Shattuck, Brookline, Massachusetts
Lent by the Massachusetts Historical Society, Boston

Peter Oliver, at his most virulent, said that John Hancock (A.B. 1754)

> was as closely attached to the hindermost Part of *Mr. Adams* as the Rattles are affixed to the Tail of the Rattle Snake. . . . His understanding was of the Dwarf Size; but his Ambition, . . . was upon the Gigantick. . . . His Mind was a meer *Tabula Rasa*, & had he met with a good Artist he would have enstamped upon it such Character as would have made him a most usefull Member of Society. But *Mr. Adams* . . . seized upon him as his Prey, & stamped such lessons upon his Mind, as have not as yet been erased.[1]

Hancock was raised by his merchant uncle Thomas Hancock, from whom he inherited one of the largest fortunes in New England. An ambitious young man, he rode through Boston in a yellow coach and at an early age dressed in the sumptuous lavender suits that would later earn him a reputation as the "Patriot in Purple."

Hancock began his political career as the protégé of Sam Adams. Called "Johnny Dupe, Esq.; alias the Milch-Cow," Hancock was young, wealthy, politically naive, and, according to John Adams, the employer of more than a thousand men in Boston.

He cooperated with the Patriots during the resistance to the Stamp Act and the creation of the non-importation agreements. When his ship "Liberty" arrived from London carrying taxable foreign wines in June 1768, shortly before the non-importation movement secured its hold over Boston, Hancock had the customs officer locked up until the cargo was unloaded. The officer's report of the incident provoked a riot in the streets of Boston. Customs officers were driven from their homes to Castle William.

And a ship belonging to Joseph Harrison (see cat. no. 79) was hauled onto Beacon Hill — near Hancock's home — and burned.

Hancock eventually broke with Adams and hewed his own erratic political course. He developed friendly relations with Governor Hutchinson for a time, but finally confirmed his allegiance to the Patriots by a fiery oration in 1774 on the anniversary of the Boston Massacre.

Thereafter he served as a representative to the Continental Congress, including a term as its president from 1775 until 1777. Hancock's preoccupation with politics and business led him to neglect Harvard College, which had named him treasurer in 1773. His refusal to account for the College's funds during the Revolutionary War (see cat. no. 49) caused Harvard great difficulties for many subsequent years.

After Hancock returned to Massachusetts from the Congress, his political skills reached maturity. His flair for popular politics and his great, although crumbling, economic power, made him Massachusetts' first governor under the new constitution. He retained that office, except for a single term, until his death in 1793.

This was not the first portrait that Copley painted of his neighbor. Hancock had commissioned the artist to paint his portrait about 1765, after he had inherited his uncle's fortune.[2] In this later painting, the figure's head and shoulders are spotlighted against a dark background, without the accoutrements associated with Copley's earlier portraits.[3]

Copley had much the same financial troubles with Hancock as did Harvard. While in Europe, the artist received the following message, dated 17 July 1774, from Henry Pelham:

> I find it very difficult collecting money. I have not yet made progress that I could wish or that you expected. Coll. Hancock I have not yet been able to gett an audience of, tho he is so well as to talk of Heading his Company in a few Days. I have always the misfortune to go there when he has a Violent Headack, or when he is laying down. . . .[4]

1. Adair and Schutz, eds., *Peter Oliver's Origins*, p. 40.
2. This painting is owned by the City of Boston.
3. Jules David Prown, *John Singleton Copley*, 1:83.
4. *Letters and Papers of John Singleton Copley and Henry Pelham, 1739-1776*, p. 232.

5. BLYTH, Benjamin (ca. 1746-after 1786), American

John Adams (1735-1826), ca. 1766

Pastel on paper. H. 58.5 x 44.5 cm.
Provenance: Thomas Boylston Adams; Elizabeth C. Adams; Charles Francis Adams II; Henry Adams; John Adams, South Lincoln, Massachusetts
Lent by the Massachusetts Historical Society, Boston

Peter Oliver considered John Adams to be "a Man of Sense," and "a Figure at the Bar," but "with an Acrimony of Temper . . ." which "settled into Rancor & Malignity." He observed that

> He was determined to raise hisself to a Superiority which he had no claim to; and he unguardedly confessed, in one of his Sallies of Pride, that *he could not bear to see anyone above him.*". . . *Mr. Adams*, being a sensible Lawyer, was for some Time, friendly to Government; . . . but Resentment drove him into every Measure subversive of Law and of Government, & interwove him with the factious Junto.[1]

Adams (A.B. 1755; honorary LL.D. 1781), coming from a family of modest means, attended Harvard on a Hollis scholarship. He thought at first of entering the ministry but, after graduation, he taught school at Worcester while studying law with James Putnam. He was admitted to the bar on 6 November 1758, the same day as his friend Samuel Quincy (cat. no. 27).

Bernard Bailyn tells us that Adams was an uneasy and driven young man, anxious and striving to achieve fame and affluence.[2] His marriage, in 1764, to Abigail Smith (cat. no. 11) afforded him greater contact with the more prominent families in the province. And the Stamp Act, in 1765, brought him into the public limelight. At first reluctant to take part in the controversy, he was drawn into the Patriots' arena and protested, with James Otis, Jr. and Jeremiah Gridley, that tax to which the colonists had never consented.

Adams' life-long dispute with Thomas Hutchinson (cat.

no. 30), then lieutenant-governor, also began to assume its mature form at this time. The monopoly of high offices by the Hutchinsons and Olivers, their friends and relatives, made Adams fear and distrust them. He perceived a conspiracy "against the public liberty," and saw Hutchinson as a power-hungry puppet, used by the ministers who, Adams thought, were destroying the British constitution. Professor Bailyn believes that it was this suspicion that brought an "ordinarily cautious man" into the "vanguard of the Revolutionary radicals."[3]

In contrast to his cousin Sam's tactics, he preferred more orderly legal arguments to prove his point. With Josiah Quincy, Jr. (cat. no. 23) and Robert Auchmuty, he defended the soldiers in the Boston Massacre trial. He served in the General Court, the Council, the Continental and Provincial Congresses, and was named chief justice of Massachusetts, though he never actually served in this last capacity.

Beginning in 1775, Adams, as "Novanglus," entered into the celebrated pamphlet debate with "Massachusettensis," whom he thought was his friend Jonathan Sewall (but was actually another friend, Daniel Leonard). John Adams lamented later that Thomas Hutchinson "seduced from his bosom three of the most intimate friends he ever had in his life — Jonathan Sewall, Samuel Quincy and Daniel Leonard — his brother barristers, his cordial and confidential friends."[4]

The Revolution launched Adams on his brilliant diplomatic and political career. He wrote the Massachusetts state constitution and served as peace commissioner to France, minister plenipotentiary to the United Provinces (Holland), and as our first ambassador to the Court of St. James. In 1788, Adams was chosen the first vice president of the United States. He served eight years in what he called "the most insignificant office that ever the invention of man contrived or his imagination conceived," until he was elected second president in 1796.

He retired, an unpopular man, to "Peacefield," his house in Quincy. Bitter against those who had opposed him, he "chewed the cud of frustration" and relived his public life in long self-justifying letters and memoirs.[5] His political wounds were deep and slow to heal, but in time he made his peace with old enemies, such as Thomas Jefferson, and settled into an honored retirement.

Benjamin Blyth was a self-taught Salem artist who specialized in pastel portraits. His advertisement in the *Salem Gazette* (10-17 May 1769) read as follows:

> Benjamin Blyth Begs Leave to inform the Public, that he has opened a Room for the Performance of Limning in Crayons at the House occupied by his Father, in the great Street leading towards Marblehead, where Specimens of his Performance may be seen. All Persons who please to favour him with their Employ, may depend upon having good likenesses and being immediately waited on, by applying to their Humble Servant, Benjamin Blyth.[6]

In addition to creating portraits in crayon of North Shore residents such as Samuel Curwen, George Cabot, and Elias Derby, he apparently assisted his brother Samuel with gilding and ornamental painting. For reasons unknown, Benjamin Blyth moved to Richmond, Virginia in 1782, where he was advertising his "limning in oil, crayons, and miniature" as late as 1786.

The Adamses visited Salem in August and November of 1766 — John on court business and Abigail probably to see her elder sister, Mary Cranch, who had recently moved to that town. Most likely, their portraits were done during these trips. The Blyth pastels — the first known portraits of the couple — are no strangers to Cambridge; they were on loan from 1935 until 1956 to Harvard, where they hung in University Hall.

---

1. Adair and Schutz, eds., *Peter Oliver's Origins*, p. 83.
2. Bernard Bailyn, "Butterfield's Adams," p. 243.
3. *Ibid.*, p. 253.
4. E. Alfred Jones, *The Loyalists of Massachusetts*, p. 242.
5. Lyman H. Butterfield et al., eds., *Diary and Autobiography of John Adams*, 1:xv.
6. Henry Wilder Foote, "Benjamin Blyth of Salem," p. 66.

6. Attributed to MAC KAY (dates unknown)

Rev. Charles Chauncy (1705-1787)

Oil on canvas. H. 87.5 x 72.5 cm.
Harvard University Portrait Collection (H 5)

The "Black Regiment" was what Oliver called the dissenting clergy, and in their ranks he included Charles Chauncy (A.B. 1721), the influential minister of Boston's First Church.

> Dr *Chauncy* was advanced in Life; he was a Man of Sense, but of exhorbitant Passions. He would utter Things in Conversation that bordered near Blasphemy; & when such wild Expressions were noticed to him, by observing that his Sermons were free from such Extravagances, he would reply, that "in making his Sermons he always kept a Blotter by him." He was of a very resentfull, unforgiving Temper; & when he was in the Excess of his Passion, a Bystander would naturally judge that he had been educated in the Purlieus of *Bedlam*; but he was open in all his Actions. His hoary Head had great Respect paid to it by the factious & seditious, & it would really have been a Crown of Glory to him had it been found in the Way of Righteousness.[1]

The Reverend Dr. Chauncy was the great-grandson of Harvard's second president, and as pastor of the First Church, he was *ex officio* a member of the Harvard Board of Overseers. After the fire of 1764, he helped with a fundraising drive to replace the lost scientific equipment.

"Charles Old Brick" was an awkward public speaker, but a distinguished scholar. In his sermons and pamphlets, he attacked both the Great Awakening and the foundation of the Church of England, the institution of bishops. His *Compleat View of Episcopacy* was long regarded as the official Congregational position toward the Anglicans.[2]

He strongly believed in the Patriot cause, working with the radicals James Otis, Jr. and Samuel Adams and giving enthusiastic and sometimes violent sermons promoting Whig issues. If their cause faltered, he thought that "a host of angels would be sent to support it."[3]

6

Very little is known about the artist MacKay (or McKay), to whom this portrait is attributed. He was active between 1788 and 1791. The American Antiquarian Society (Worcester, Massachusetts) owns two portraits painted by him in 1791, those of John and Hannah Bush.

---

1. Adair and Schutz, eds., *Peter Oliver's Origins,* p. 43.
2. *Sibley's,* 6:447-48.
3. *Ibid.,* p. 451.

7. Attributed to GREENWOOD, John (1727-1792), American

Rev. Jonathan Mayhew (1720-1766), ca. 1750

Oil on canvas. H. 74.9 x 57.8 cm.
Provenance: Ralph Dunning
Lent by the Congregational Library, Boston, Massachusetts

Jonathan Mayhew (A.B. 1744) was

> a Man of Sense, but . . . very slow in arranging & consolidating his Ideas. In Conversation he was an awkard Disputant, as well as in his extempore Pulpit Effusions. Both were more like to the Water of a River dashing over the Rocks that impeded its Course, than to the smooth flowing Current. Both were so unharmonious and discordant, that they always grated upon the Ears of his Auditors; but his polemick Performances, although elaborate & inelegant, showed Strength of Reason. He had too great a Share of Pride for an humble Disciple of so divine a Master, & looked with too contemptuous an Eye on all around him.[1]

Thus did Peter Oliver sum up one of Boston's most radical Congregational ministers.

The son of Experience and Remember Mayhew, Jonathan came from a family of missionaries who preached to the Indians on Martha's Vineyard, which had been given to his family in a land grant in 1641. Entering Harvard at a relatively late age, when he was almost twenty-one, Mayhew received both Hollis and Danforth scholarships, but he was undisciplined and frequently fined for unruly behavior. His studies became more serious after he experienced the Great Awakening — English evangelist George Whitefield's religious revival — and decided to become a minister.

Mayhew was a resident graduate of Harvard from 1744 until 1747, when he became the pastor of the West Church in Boston. His congregation was composed largely of wealthy merchants, and included such liberals as James Otis, Jr., Sam Adams, James Bowdoin, and John Win-

throp. Mayhew's outspoken rejection of New England's Calvinist tradition caused the majority of Boston's clergy to shun him.

Mayhew was equally direct on political matters. His major political statement, *A Discourse Concerning Unlimited Submission and Non-Resistance to Higher Powers* (1750), explained the Whig justification for resistance to

higher authority and attacked the Anglican devotion to the "martyred" Charles I.

The sermon attracted the attention of a self-described "lover of liberty," the wealthy English gentleman, Thomas Hollis V (cat. nos. 87-90). Hollis was inspired to send Mayhew a copy of Algernon Sidney's works, and, for over a decade, he continued to ship selected libertarian volumes to the New England pastor. He was also responsible for publishing Mayhew's sermons in England, where Jonathan soon became famous, and he put Mayhew in contact with other English radicals. But Mayhew could not convince Hollis to take an active or public role in the Patriots' cause.

Mayhew, already a controversial figure, led the Congregationalists' attack on the Anglicans in 1763 (see cat. no. 17). But soon more strictly political crises were preoccupying the radical pastor. Some of his fiery sermons were said to have incited riots, including the one which destroyed Thomas Hutchinson's house in 1765; Tory members of the congregation, such as Richard Clarke (see cat. no. 42), withdrew from the church.

Yet Mayhew was deeply shocked by this violence. He wrote to Hutchinson: "God is my witness, that from the bottom of my heart I detest these proceedings; . . . And, in truth, I had rather lose my hand than be an encourager of such outrages as were committed last night."[2]

At the repeal of the Stamp Act, Mayhew's congregation asked him to write a thanksgiving sermon. *The Snare Broken*, delivered on 23 May 1766, was the most widely read of the hundreds of sermons prepared for that joyous occasion. His inspiration came from Psalms 123:7-8, "Our soul is escaped as a bird from the snare of fowlers; the snare is broken, and we are escaped. . . ."[3] Rev. Mayhew told his congregation that the colonies

are emancipated from a slavish, inglorious bondage; are re-instated in the enjoyment of their ancient rights and privileges, and a foundation is laid for lasting harmony between Great Britain and them, to their mutual advantage.[4]

Mayhew's optimism proved unjustified, but he did not live to see it shattered. He died 9 July 1766, ten years before the Revolution.

John Greenwood, the son of a wealthy and cultured Boston family, was apprenticed to Thomas Johnston — heraldic artist, engraver, japanner, and ornamental artist — shortly after his father's death in 1742. By 1745, the tall, handsome Greenwood had begun to paint portraits of Boston's clergy, merchants, and teachers. His reputation for strong, linear portraits, such as this one, was soon known in England.

He was in Surinam (Dutch Guiana) from 1752 to 1758 painting portraits, and in Holland from 1758 to 1762, studying the art of mezzotint engraving. In 1762 he moved to London and established himself as a scrupulous art dealer, buying and selling for such clients as the earl of Bute and the estate of William Hogarth.[5] He continued to paint for a few years, until his business required almost all of his time.

A successful man, he did not forget Harvard College, where his father and half-brother had received their education and where his uncle Isaac served as Hollis Professor of Mathematics and Natural Philosophy. He sent the College in 1769 "two curious Egyptian mummies," which apparently no longer exist.

---

1. Adair and Schutz, eds., *Peter Oliver's Origins*, p. 43.
2. Bernard Bailyn, "Religion and Revolution," 4:115.
3. Charles W. Akers, *Called Unto Liberty*, p. 212.
4. *Ibid.*, p. 212.
5. Alan Burroughs, *John Greenwood in America 1745-1752*, p. 51.

8. COPLEY, John Singleton (1738-1815), American

Rev. Samuel Cooper (1725-1783), 1769-71

Oil on canvas. H. 74.8 x 62.2 cm.
Provenance: Marvin C. Taylor, Boston, a direct descendant of the sitter; Charles M. Davenport, Boston
Lent by Williams College Museum of Art

"No man," said Oliver of Rev. Samuel Cooper (A.B. 1743), "could, with a better Grace, utter the word of *God* from his Mouth, & at the same time keep a two edged Dagger concealed in his Hand."

> His Tongue was Butter & Oil, but under it was the poison of Asps. . . . He could not only prevaricate with Man, but with *God* also; . . . The Fluency of his Tongue & the Ease of his Manner, were such, that he was always agreeable to the politest Company, who were unacquainted with his real Character; & he could descend from them to mix privately with the Rabble, in their nightly seditious Associations.[1]

Cooper was only twenty-one years of age when members of the wealthy, liberal Brattle Street Church named him their parson, a position his father, William Cooper, had held previously. "Silver-Tongued Sam" was adept at mixing religion and politics.

He began his active political career during the excise controversy of 1754. While serving as chaplain to the House of Representatives, he published an anonymous pamphlet, *The Crisis*, against the proposed tax on wine and rum. It is said that as the war approached he frequently sent substitute preachers into his church so that he could attend clandestine meetings in the parsonage with Otis, Hancock, and Sam Adams. He made many contributions to the Revolution, helping John Hancock prepare public statements, introducing Lafayette to Franklin, and working to convince the French to assist the colonies.

Cooper was active in the affairs of Harvard College, as both an overseer and member of the Corporation. He was

elected president of the College in 1774, but declined the office.

In 1775 he fled Boston, frightened by the warrants for the arrest of Whig leaders issued by the British. He returned after the evacuation in 1776 and moved into a luxurious home furnished with confiscated Tory goods. Cooper continued preaching and, in 1777, delivered Boston's first official Fourth of July sermon. He suffered a mental breakdown in 1783, brought on, it was said, by an excessive use of Scottish snuff.[2]

Rev. Samuel Cooper presided at the marriage of Susanna Clarke and John Singleton Copley on 16 November 1769. Reportedly, this portrait, painted by Copley, was damaged by the bayonets of British soldiers during the siege of Boston.[3]

1. Adair and Schutz, eds., *Peter Oliver's Origins,* pp. 44-45.
2. *Sibley's,* 11:211.
3. Barbara N. Parker and Anne B. Wheeler, *John Singleton Copley in America,* p. 62.

9. COPLEY, John Singleton (1738-1815), American

Mercy Otis Warren (Mrs. James Warren, 1728-1814), ca. 1763

Oil on canvas. H. 130.1 x 104.1 cm.
Provenance: Winslow Warren, descendant of the sitter, Dedham, Massachusetts
Lent by the Museum of Fine Arts, Boston; bequest of Winslow Warren (31.212)

Mercy Otis Warren, sister of the radical James Otis, Jr., was exposed to politics and the Whig philosophy from birth. With her marriage in 1754 to James Warren, a Patriot merchant and farmer, her interest in political affairs increased. Their home in Plymouth fast became a meeting place for the rebel leaders, and Mercy, it is said, took an active part in forming the plans that originated there.

With encouragement from her husband and their good friend John Adams, Warren began writing anonymous political plays which espoused the Patriot cause. Her first attempt, *The Adulateur*, appeared in 1772 in the *Massachusetts Spy* and satirized the monopoly of offices by Thomas Hutchinson and his relatives. The publication of the Hutchinson-Oliver Letters (cat. no. 32) in 1773 inspired *The Defeat*, her second play. Her most popular political satire, however, was *The Group* (cat. no. 10), which appeared in 1775.

During the Revolution she continued to pen political plays and poetry and to care for her five sons while her husband James attended to his duties as president of the Continental Congress and paymaster for the troops in Concord and Watertown. She passed some of the lonely hours visiting and corresponding with her friend Abigail Adams, who was close by in Braintree.

In 1781 the Warrens purchased a new house in Milton; ironically, it was the estate of former governor Thomas Hutchinson. There they entertained such distinguished guests as Lafayette and Jefferson. But "Milton Hall" proved to be too expensive, and around 1788 they returned to Plymouth.

Shortly following the close of the Revolution, Warren

began work on her three-volume *History of the Rise, Progress, and Termination of the American Revolution.* Published in 1805, it equalled Peter Oliver's account in its partisanship. She painted Gov. Thomas Hutchinson as "dark, intriguing, insinuating, haughty, and ambitious."[1] Chief Justice Peter Oliver emerged as an ignorant, unprincipled partisan, willing to use his office to sanction "the most atrocious acts of arbitrary power. . . ."[2]

Sam Adams, on the other hand, possessed "a quick understanding, a cool head, stern manners, a smooth address, and a Roman-like firmness, united with . . . sagacity and penetration. . . ."[3] And the hero of the piece was her brother, James Otis, Jr. who "may justly claim the honor of laying the foundation of a revolution. . . . He was the first champion of American freedom. . . . His humanity was conspicuous, his sincerity acknowledged, his integrity unimpeached, his honor unblemished, and his patriotism marked with the disinterestedness of the Spartan."[4]

The Adamses and Warrens had begun to part ways shortly after the Revolution — the former were Federalists and the latter anti-Federalists.[5] Warren's *History*, in which John Adams was described as a man whose "passions and prejudices were sometimes too strong for his sagacity and judgment,"[6] further weakened the friendship. Adams, who had encouraged Mercy to undertake her account, now remarked that "History is not the Province of the Ladies," and a bitter quarrel ensued. The argument was ended in 1813, with the help of Elbridge Gerry; John, Abigail, and Mercy exchanged locks of their hair in friendship.

1. Mercy Otis Warren, *History of the Rise, Progress, and Termination of the American Revolution,* 1:79.
2. *Ibid.,* p. 119.
3. *Ibid.,* pp. 210-11.
4. *Ibid.,* pp. 47, 85.
5. Mercy Warren expressed some of her anti-Federalist views in a volume entitled *Observations on the New Constitution,* published in 1788.
6. Mercy Otis Warren, *History,* 3:392.

10. [Warren, Mercy Otis]
The Group

Boston: Edes and Gill, 1775. H. 19.5 cm.
Lent by the Houghton Library; gift of Ernest Blaney Dane
  (*AC7.W2537.775g)

The first part of *The Group* appeared in the *Boston Gazette,* a Patriot newspaper,[1] on 23 January 1775 and in the *Massachusetts Spy* three days later. Mercy Otis Warren finished the second act by 15 March. But by then the papers were full of news about the mounting tensions between Britain and her colonies. Boston's printers had no space for plays — not even political satires blasting the royal government. *The Group* did appear in pamphlet form, however, published on 3 April 1775 by Edes and Gill, who advertised it for "9 coppers." It was subsequently reissued in both New York and Philadelphia.

The "group" referred to in the title was the Mandamus Council, appointed by the crown in August 1774 to replace the traditional governor's Council under a provision of the Intolerable Acts that Warren dubbed "a burlesque on good government."[2]

As the play opens, the councillors have gathered in Boston to discuss the current crisis and to ask the British for protection from the mobs. There is little action, only conversation (in blank verse) among the characters.

Contemporary figures and later historians alike have ascribed names to the councillors satirized in this play. Listed below are the characters and their identities:

Lord Chief Justice Halzerod	Peter Oliver
Judge Meagae	Foster Hutchinson
Brigadier Hateall	Timothy Ruggles
Hum Humbug, Esq.	John Erving, Jr.
Sir Sparrow Spendall	Sir William Pepperrell
Hector Mushroom, Col.	Col. Murray
Beau Trumps	Daniel Leonard
Dick, the Publican	Richard Lechmere

Simple Sapling, Esq.	Nathaniel Ray Thomas
Monsieur de François	James Boutineau
Crusty Crowbar	Josiah Edson
Dupe, Secretary of State	Thomas Flucker
Scriblerius Fribble	Harrison Gray(?)
Commodore Batteau	Joshua Loring
Collateralis, a new made judge	William Browne

John Adams, on receiving a copy of *The Group,* had written to Mercy Warren:

> I was charmed by three characters drawn by a most masterly Pen. . . . Copley's Pencil could not have touched off with more exquisite Finishings the Faces of these Gentlemen. . . . You Ladies are the most infallible judges of Characters, I think.[2]

It was to Adams that Warren turned for help when the authorship of the play was questioned. In 1814, a friend had seen at the Boston Athenaeum a copy of this play, with a statement ascribing it to the pen of Samuel Barrett. Adams personally went to the Athenaeum (where the copy may still be found) and wrote at the end of the play:

> Quincy August 17. 1814. The "Group," to my certain knowledge was written by Mrs Mercy Warren of Plymouth. So certifies John Adams.

Although the title page states that *The Group* is a farce, "As lately Acted, and to be Re-acted, to the Wonder of all Superior Intelligences, Nigh Headquarters, at Amboyne," none of Mercy Otis Warren's political satires were ever performed, nor did she probably ever intend them to be. They were morality plays, pieces of Patriot propaganda, meant to be read for the "lessons" they contained.

---

1. Some of the first essays by James Otis, Jr., Jonathan Mayhew, Josiah Quincy, Jr., and Samuel Cooper appeared in the *Boston Gazette,* "celebrated for the freedom of its disquisitors in favor of civil liberty." Mercy Otis Warren said, "the paper became odious to the friends of prerogative, but not more disgusting to the tories and high church than it was pleasing to the Whigs" (Warren, *History,* 1:84). The paper was founded in 1755 and published by Benjamin Edes and John Gill, whose arrest for instigating sedition

DRAMATIS PERSONÆ

Lord Chief Justice HALZEROD,
Judge MEAGAE,
Brigadier HATEALL,
HUM HUMBUG, Esq;
Sir SPARROW SPENDALL,
HECTOR MUSHROOM,——Col.
BEAU TRUMPS,
DICK, the Publican,
SIMPLE SAPLING, Esq;
Monsieur de FRANCOIS,
CRUSTY CROWBAR, Esq;
DUPE,——Secretary of State,
SCRIBLERIUS FRIBBLE,
COMMODORE BATTEAU,
COLLATERALIS,——a new made Judge.

Attended by a swarm of court sycophants, hungry harpies, and unprincipled danglers, collected from the neighbouring villages, hovering over the stage in the shape of locusts, led by Massachusettensis in the form of a basilisk ; the rear brought up by proteus, bearing a torch in one hand, and a powder-flask in the other : The whole supported by a mighty army and navy, from blunderland, for the laudible purpose of enslaving its best friends.

was suggested by Gov. Bernard. Revolutionary leaders held private meetings in the upstairs "Long Room" of Edes and Gill, and the Patriots reportedly donned their Indian disguises there before the Boston Tea Party. During the siege of Boston, Edes and Gill set up shop in Charlestown and continued to print their paper.

2. Maud Macdonald Hutcheson, "Mercy Warren, 1728-1814," p. 387.
3. *Warren-Adams Letters*, 1:201. John Adams to Mercy Otis Warren, 8 January 1776.
4. *Ibid.*, 2:396. John Adams to Mercy Otis Warren, 17 August 1814.

11. BLYTH, Benjamin (ca. 1749-after 1786), American

Abigail Smith Adams (Mrs. John Adams, 1744-1818), ca. 1766

Pastel on paper. H. 58.5 x 44.5 cm.
Provenance: Thomas Boylston Adams; Elizabeth C. Adams; Charles Francis Adams; Henry Adams; John Adams, South Lincoln, Massachusetts
Lent by the Massachusetts Historical Society, Boston

Abigail Smith Adams was the daughter of Rev. William Smith of Weymouth and Elizabeth Quincy of Braintree. Like her friend, Mercy Otis Warren (cat. no. 9), Abigail received no formal schooling, but was an avid reader and taught herself many of the basics. She met John Adams when she was eighteen, and married him by the time she reached age twenty.

For the first ten years of their marriage — which yielded five children — the Adamses lived in a farmhouse in Braintree, and in Boston. But in 1774 John Adams left for Philadelphia and the Continental Congress. They were to be separated for most of the second decade of their marriage. Abigail was left to educate the children, manage the farm, and support their family.

Although John and Abigail could seldom be together, their relationship continued with lively letters on every imaginable subject. She often included her political advice, as when she lobbied for women's rights on 31 March 1776:

> And, by the way, in the new code of laws which I suppose it will be necessary for you to make, I desire you would remember the ladies and be more generous and favorable to them than your ancestors: Do not put such unlimited power into the hands of the husbands. Remember, all men would be tyrants if they could. If particular care and attention is not paid to the ladies, we are determined to foment a rebellion, and will not hold ourselves bound by any laws in which we have no voice or representation.[1]

John Adams replied that her letter "was the first intimation" that a "tribe, more numerous and powerful than all the rest, were grown discontented," but added that men knew better than to repeal the "masculine systems."[2]

She often confessed her loneliness to her friend "Marcia" Warren, who had also been separated from her husband due to the war:

> I am curious to know how you spend your time? . . . I hope soon to have the pleasure of seeing you at Braintree and of a social evening beside our fire. How happy should I esteem myself could the dear Friend of my Heart join us. I think I make a greater sacrifice to the publick than I could by Gold and Silver, had I it to bestow. Does not Marcia join in this sentiment with her [?] Portia.[3]

"Portia" was to leave the quiet New England existence behind to accompany John Adams as he served in various posts in Europe — to The Hague, Paris, and London. She clearly missed Massachusetts, however, and told Thomas Jefferson that she preferred her Braintree farm to "the Court of St. James's where I seldom meet with characters so innofensive as my Hens and chickings, or minds so well improved as my garden."[4]

But it was not until 1801, after her husband had served as both vice president and president, that she could quietly retire to the countryside of Quincy, Massachusetts. There she read and continued her correspondence and delighted in her grandchildren, until she died of a fever in 1818.

Abigail's strength of character is reflected in her portrait by Benjamin Blyth. While Bernard Bailyn notes that the companion portrait of John Adams (see cat. no. 5) depicts "a likable but unimpressive face: round, rather soft-looking, bland, and withdrawn," he finds Abigail's face "extraordinary, not so much for its beauty, which, in a masculine way, is clearly enough there, as for the maturity and the power of personality it expresses."[5]

1. Charles Francis Adams, ed., *Familiar Letters of John Adams and His Wife Abigail Adams, During the Revolution,* pp. 149-50.

2. *Ibid.,* p. 155.

3. *Warren-Adams Letters,* 1:179-81. Abigail Adams to Mercy Otis Warren, November 1775.

4. Edward T. James, ed., *Notable American Women,* 1:8. Abigail Adams to Thomas Jefferson, 26 February 1788.

5. Bailyn, "Butterfield's Adams," pp. 249-50.

12. COPLEY, John Singleton (1738-1815), American

Dorothy Quincy (later Mrs. John Hancock; Mrs. James Scott, 1747-1830), ca. 1772

Oil on canvas. H. 127 x 99 cm.
Provenance: Theodore Cushing of Little Harbor, New Hampshire; Harriet A. Cushing (1873); Mrs. George S. Rose (1895); Mrs. Atherton Loring, her granddaughter
Lent by the Museum of Fine Arts, Boston; Charles H. Bayley Fund and partial gift of Anne B. Loring (1975.13)

Dorothy Quincy was the youngest of many children in the family of Edmund and Elizabeth (Wendell) Quincy. She grew up in Braintree, near her Quincy cousins — Samuel, Hannah, Josiah, Jr., and Edmund III. During the Revolution she lived for a time with Lydia Hancock (John Hancock's aunt) in Lexington, and later stayed with Aaron Burr's brother Thaddeus in Fairfield, Connecticut. On 28 August 1775 while the First Continental Congress was in recess, "Dolly" married the Patriot John Hancock. (Her sister, Esther, had married a Tory, Jonathan Sewall, in 1764.)

After the war, the Hancocks lived on a Beacon Hill estate while Hancock served as Massachusetts' first governor. Dorothy was the town's most prominent hostess, continuously entertaining Boston society. When the governor died in 1793, he left her a mountain of debts and limited means with which to meet them. She married Col. James Scott and moved to his home in Portsmouth, New Hampshire. After Scott's death in 1809, she returned to Boston where she lived quietly until her death in 1830.[1]

This three-quarter length portrait is very similar in pose and costume to that of her cousin, Dorothy Wendell Skinner, also painted by Copley and dated 1772.

---

1. *Sibley's,* 13:445.

13. Attributed to ATKINS, Gibbs (1739-1806), American

Secretary, Boston, ca. 1770-76

Mahogany and white pine. H. 254 (without center finial), W. 119.5,
    D. 60.5 cm.
Provenance: Descendants of Martin Gay
Lent by Ebenezer Gay

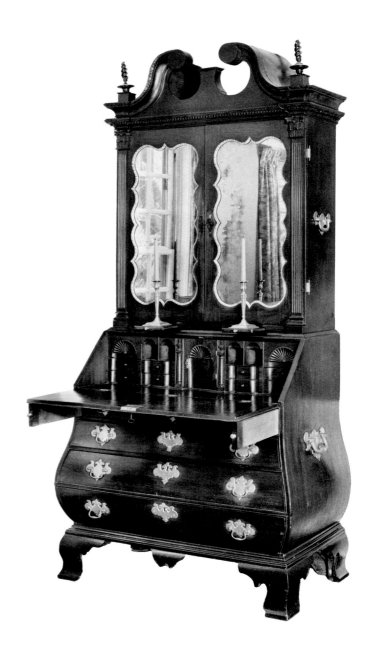

This bombé secretary was built for Capt. Martin Gay
(1726-1809) of Boston, a brass founder and coppersmith.
When General Howe and his British soldiers evacuated
Boston in 1776, Martin Gay was among the Loyalists who
accompanied them to Halifax. He took his daughter
Mary, his son Martin, "his man London," and this mahogany secretary, which is nicknamed the "Old Tory."[1]
In the drawers of the secretary were placed linen and a
silver communion service from the West Church. Gay, as
deacon, had been asked to protect the church's valuables,
since the meetinghouse was about to be used as barracks
for the British troops.

Most Loyalists took only silver and other portable
objects when they fled, because of lack of space on the
king's ships. Martin Gay had his own vessel and thus was
able to carry this large piece of furniture with him. Never-
theless, it is interesting that he did not choose to leave
so bulky an object with his second wife, Ruth, who, like
many Loyalists' wives, remained in Boston to protect her
husband's property from the threat of confiscation.[2]

Martin Gay's exile in Nova Scotia and London came
to an end in 1792, when he returned to Boston with the
"Old Tory," the communion service still in its drawers.
Ruth — who might well have spent the war years with
her family, most of whom were Patriots — had shrewdly
managed to maintain most of her husband's property, so
Martin was able to resume his business as a coppersmith.

Ruth's brother, Gibbs Atkins, a cabinetmaker, probably
crafted this combination desk and bookcase and pre-

sented it to the Gays as a wedding present.[3] Like Martin Gay, Atkins left for Halifax in 1776, but returned after the war. He was one of only six cabinetmakers in Boston to produce bombé furniture.

Bombé furniture, characterized by a swelling or bulge near the base, was popular in Boston for over fifty years, although the style did not spread to other colonies. The wealthy, social families — Quincy, Hutchinson, Apthorp, Vassall — kept up with the fashions of the mother country and owned bombé (also called "kettle shape") pieces such as this one, inspired by the graceful curvilinear Baroque style so prominent in England at this time.[4]

The base of the finials and the gilded eagle were removed (see illustration) to fit the secretary into the owner's home. These have been returned to the secretary for this exhibition.

1. Mabel M. Swan, "Furniture of the Boston Tories," p. 187.
2. For the history of Ruth Gay's attempts to save the property, see Edward Wheelwright, "Three Letters Written by an American Loyalist to his Wife, 1775-1778," in *Publications of the Colonial Society of Massachusetts*, 3(1895-97):379-400.
3. Swan, "Furniture of the Boston Tories," p. 187.
4. Gilbert T. Vincent, "The Bombé Furniture of Boston," in *Boston Furniture of the Eighteenth Century*, pp. 137-196.

II. Harvard Divided, *Mayhew-Apthorp Debate*

Following the death in February 1763 of Dr. Ebenezer Miller, the Anglican rector in Braintree, Massachusetts, anonymous letters and articles appeared in the *Boston Gazette* ridiculing the work of the Society for the Propagation of the Gospel in Foreign Parts (S.P.G.). The editorials accused the S.P.G. of attempting to convert the dissenters rather than the "savages." The natives of Braintree were afraid, the writer suggested, that without a missionary among them they might "relapse into the same *savage* and *barbarous* state, in which they were before there was an Episcopal Minister settled there."[1]

Although the articles were signed "T.L.," Jonathan Mayhew (cat. nos. 7 and 17), an arch-opponent of Anglicanism, was accused of being responsible for them. Mayhew had heard rumors from Thomas Hollis (cat. nos. 87-90), in London, that a bishop might be sent to America. Indeed, as Bernard Bailyn has noted, this threat was very real to Mayhew and his fellow dissenters. Anglican leaders in New York and New Jersey had petitioned the mother country for an episcopate in the colonies.[2] They needed a bishop who could confirm, ordain, and carry out other official duties. But bishops were also imperial placemen, with great political as well as religious authority.

East Apthorp (cat. no. 14), the rector of a new mission in Cambridge, Christ Church (cat. no. 79), wrote the principal defense of the S.P.G. His *Considerations on the Institution and Conduct of the Society for the Propagation of the Gospel in Foreign Parts* (cat. no. 16), appearing in March 1763, upheld the Society's right to send missionaries wherever they were requested. Professor Bailyn feels this pamphlet by the "inexperienced, contentious, and supercilious" Apthorp only reinforced the fears of an American episcopate.[3] Apthorp was regarded as a spy for the Archbishop of Canterbury. His church, in full view of that bastion of Congregationalism, Harvard College, was considered another symbol of creeping British imperial control. And he used his family's fortune to build Apthorp House (see cat. no. 15), hardly the simple dwelling of a missionary. To Jonathan Mayhew, it was a "Bishop's Palace."

Jonathan Mayhew's tract *Observations on the Charter and Conduct of the Society for the Propagation of the Gospel . . . With Remarks on the Mistakes of East Apthorp* questioned the right of the S.P.G. to send a missionary to a town such as Cambridge which had ample pastors and meetinghouses. Indeed, said Mayhew, the S.P.G. should turn its attention to the Indians and Negroes who need its proselytizing. The two denominations should not set up "altar against altar."

> Will they never let us rest in peace . . . ? Is it not enough, that they persecuted us out of the old world? Will they pursue us unto the new to convert us here, . . . while they neglect the heathen and heathenish plantations! What other new world remains as a sanctuary for us from their oppressions, in case of need? Where is the COLUMBUS to explore one for, and pilot us to it, before we are consumed by the flames, or deluged in a flood of episcopacy?[4]

But the issue went beyond religious freedom. According to Mayhew, the king and his Parliament had no right to establish their religion or to interfere in any way with the colonies' business.[5] The Anglican Church (and its S.P.G.) was a part of the English state, and its missionaries were seen as agents of the royal government. Some New Englanders saw the establishment of Christ Church, built under the S.P.G.'s aegis, as a symbol of the crown's increasing aggression and its attempts to curtail their rights and liberties. To them, the "episcopizing" of America was but a different part of the same conspiracy.[6]

East Apthorp was not so quick to reply this time, but the Anglicans had others to pick up the gauntlet. A pamphlet from Providence, Rhode Island, censured Mayhew for his ingratitude to England; another from Portsmouth, New Hampshire, continued the personal attack on Rev. Jonathan Mayhew.

In October 1763 Henry Caner, rector of King's Chapel in Boston and the man most likely to be appointed bishop, wrote (anonymously) *A Candid Examination of Dr. Mayhew's Remarks*. He argued that the Church of England was the established religion in New England and threatened royal action against the enemies of Anglicanism.[7] Appended to it was a *Letter to a Friend* (written by Dr. Samuel Johnson) which tried to convince readers that an American bishop would be no threat to the colonists' liberties.[8] Mayhew's *A Defence of the Observations* was a reply to both Caner and Johnson.

The spring of 1764 brought the pamphlet of an "English writer," known to be the Archbishop of Canterbury himself: the *Answer to Dr. Mayhew's Observations*. Thomas Secker's participation indicates the importance of Mayhew's challenge. The debate was followed as closely in the mother country as in New England. Thomas Hollis made sure that the pamphlets were reprinted and distributed in England, and the papers were filled with news of the controversy.

Remarks on an Anonymous Tract (cat. no. 18) was Mayhew's reply to Secker's pamphlet. He reiterated his "entering wedge" argument: the feeling that once one bishop was established in America, others would follow, and they would have increasing political as well as religious powers over the colonists. Nations, he reminded Secker, were usually deprived of their liberties gradually.

Finally, writing from England in 1764, East Apthorp—who was the only Anglican to write under his own name—had the last word in *A Review of Dr. Mayhew's Remarks on the Answer....* It concluded with the statement that "the advancement of the Church of England is for the interest of Truth, Order and reasonable Liberty."[9]

Here the debate ended. With passage of the Stamp Act in 1765, secular matters came to provide the ammunition for the dispute between Britain and her colonies.

---

1. Charles W. Akers, *Called Unto Liberty*, p. 180.
2. Bernard Bailyn, *The Ideological Origins of the American Revolution*, p. 96.
3. *Ibid.*, p. 254.
4. Akers, *Called Unto Liberty*, p. 184.
5. Bailyn, *Ideological Origins*, p. 256.
6. *Ibid.*, p. 97.
7. Akers, *Called Unto Liberty*, pp. 187-88.
8. Sam Johnson requested that the Archbishop of Canterbury give an honorary doctorate to Caner, in order to increase the prestige of the Church of England in Massachusetts. The Congregationalists already had three Doctors of Divinity. In 1765 Oxford conferred degrees on Caner and two other prominent New England Anglicans.
9. Akers, *Called Unto Liberty*, p. 195.

East Apthorp.

14. Artist Unknown

East Apthorp (1733-1816)

Silhouette (reproduction). H. 17 x 11 cm.
Lent by Apthorp House

Rev. East Apthorp came from one of Boston's wealthiest merchant families. He attended Jesus College, Cambridge, until 1759 when his studies in classics and religion were interrupted by news of his father's death, and he returned to Boston.

At twenty-six years of age, he was given the choice of becoming vice president of King's College (now Columbia) or rector of the newly founded Christ Church in Cambridge, Massachusetts. He accepted the latter offer.

Christ Church opened its doors in 1761. That same year, East Apthorp and his wife, Elizabeth Hutchinson, moved into their luxurious house facing the Charles River. Apthorp's tenure was peaceful until 1763, when the pamphlet war began between the Anglicans and Congregationalists.

In 1764, Apthorp requested the S.P.G. to grant him a leave of absence in order that he might visit England to continue studies and to attend to various business matters. He never returned to Massachusetts. Apthorp lived in England, preaching in Croydon and London, writing books and pamphlets on history and classics, until his death in 1816.

15A. GRIFFIN, Samuel (1762-1812), American

A Westerly Perspective of Part of the Town of Cambridge, 1783-84

Pen, ink, and watercolor on white laid paper. H. 14.6 x 32.2 cm.
Inscribed, in ink or scroll, u.l.: A westerly perspective / VIEW / of part of the town of / Cambridge; l.l. margin, in a later hand: By Samuel Griffin, class of 1784
Inscribed, in ink on reverse, u.r.: Cambridge, Mass. 1783.
Lent by Harvard University Archives; gift of Commodore T. D. Griffin, U.S. Navy, 1917 (HUV 2183pf)

B. **Apthorp House,** November 1975
Photograph. H. 28 x 35 cm.
Paul Birnbaum, photographer

In 1760 construction began on a house for East Apthorp, who had purchased about six acres of land facing the Charles River. Work progressed simultaneously with that of Christ Church. Both were completed in 1761.

The Mayhew-Apthorp debate brought the mansion into the limelight and made it a controversial issue. It soon became known as the "Bishop's Palace," with the Congregationalists wondering aloud how a humble missionary with an income of £20 sterling per year could afford to build such a magnificent home. Mayhew reported in his *Observations*, ". . . It is supposed by many, that a certain *superb edifice* in a neighbouring town, was even from the foundation designed for the *Palace* of one of the *humble successors* of the apostles."[1] He repeated his suspicions in the later *Remarks on an Anonymous Tract* (see cat. no. 18). But Apthorp House was never intended to be a parsonage; it was the home of an heir to a great New England fortune.

The grand house, with its Palladian proportion and symmetry and classical details, has been attributed to the architect of Christ Church, Peter Harrison (see cat. no. 79), who was a friend and business associate of the Apthorps and other leading Anglicans.[2]

The second owner of Apthorp House, the merchant

John Borland, added a third story in 1771. A Tory whose wife was a cousin of the Vassalls, Borland fled Cambridge in 1775, and the house was confiscated by the Committee of Safety which, in turn, leased it to Col. David Henley.

The house was looted and then used as a barracks for troops. Gen. Israel Putnam and his officers stayed there before the battle of Bunker Hill. During the winter of 1777-1778 Henley rented the house for the exorbitant sum of £150 to Gen. John Burgoyne, whose men had surrendered at Saratoga and were awaiting transport from Boston back to England.

In the early nineteenth century, Apthorp House was used to board clergymen and Harvard instructors. It later became "Apthorp College," one of the private dormitories formed in the Gold Coast days. Sold to Harvard in 1916, it served as living quarters for undergraduates. And, with the creation of the house system in 1930, it became the residence of the master of Adams House.

This view depicts the area around Harvard in 1783-1784. The buildings, beginning at left, are: Apthorp House; First Church (cat. no. 81); Wadsworth House (cat. no. 43); Wigglesworth House Sewall House; the Parsonage; Christ Church (cat. no. 79); Massachusetts, Harvard and Hollis Halls; and a group of houses on what was later called Holmes Place (Oliver Wendell Holmes, Sr. was born there in 1809) which is now part of the Law School. Between Harvard and Massachusetts Halls lies a summerhouse (on what was formerly a part of the John Vassall estate), and, beside Hollis, is the College's brewhouse, barn, and pigsty.[3] This view is somewhat confusing, since the artist did not include Braintree Street (now Massachusetts Avenue), and the houses which were actually on the other side of the street look as if they are part of the College.

The view was drawn by Samuel Griffin, a native of Kingston, New Hampshire, either for his commencement thesis or the Exhibition held in April 1784. After graduation, he studied medicine with Dr. Edward Holyoke of Salem, and then moved to Virginia, where he was reportedly killed by one of his wife's slaves in 1812.[4]

The view was part of a mathematical notebook kept by Griffin while at Harvard. Griffin compiled many watercolor sketches illustrating the problems of surveying and perspective, as well as notes on navigation, geometry, and trigonometry. Most likely he was forced to keep this notebook by the shortage of regular textbooks during and immediately after the revolutionary era.

1. Wendell Garrett, *Apthorp House, 1760-1960*, p. 16.
2. *Ibid.*, p. 26.
3. Hamilton Vaughan Bail, *Views of Harvard*, p. 77.
4. *Ibid.*, p. 78.

16. Apthorp, East

Considerations on the Institution and Conduct of the Society for the Propagation of the Gospel in Foreign Parts . . .

Boston: Green & Russell, 1763. H. 20.5 cm.
Lent by the Houghton Library; gift of John Holmes, 1870
(*AC7.AP846.763c)

In his *Considerations* East Apthorp cited the Charter of the Society for the Propagation of the Gospel in Foreign Parts to prove that the S.P.G.'s purpose was first of all to maintain public worship for English subjects in the colonies and secondarily to convert the heathens. Apthorp believed "that this truly *Christian* society, the honour of our age and nation, cannot better apply their munificence, than in providing, throughout our Colonies, for the decent celebration of our public Religion."[1]

At the end of this volume, Rev. East Apthorp apologized for taking time to reply to Rev. Jonathan Mayhew, promising in the future to use his studies for better purposes. Following his return to England, however, Apthorp did review the entire controversy in 1765, with the publication of *A Review of Dr. Mayhew's Remarks on the Answer to his Observations. . . .* Mayhew did not answer this last pamphlet in their debate.

---

1. Missionaries were never sent unless requested, as had been the case at Cambridge.

CONSIDERATIONS

ON THE

INSTITUTION and CONDUCT

OF THE

SOCIETY FOR THE PROPAGATION

OF THE

GOSPEL IN FOREIGN PARTS.

By *EAST APTHORP*, M. A.

MISSIONARY AT CAMBRIDGE.

Cum res *illi* suas, quibus utique notiores eæ sunt, accurate planeque doceant; *hi* vero quasdam tantum iis de rebus suspiciones, quas minime perspectas habent, in absurdas ac futiles disputationum ineptias conferant: *utris* obsecro fidem habendam esse ratio suadeat? imó, indignum certe fuerit, vel hoc quærere. Vanos continuó ac mendaces esse, qui eas respuunt, necesse est.
EUSEB. Præp. Evang. l. III. c. 15. ex
vers. Vigeri.

BOSTON, NEW-ENGLAND:
Printed by GREEN & RUSSELL, in Queen-Street,
and THOMAS & JOHN FLEET, in Cornhill.
MDCCLXIII.

IONATHAN MAYHEW, D·D·PASTOR OF THE WEST CHVRCH
IN BOSTON, IN NEW ENGLAND, AN ASSERTOR OF THE CIVIL
AND RELIGIOVS LIBERTIES OF HIS COVNTRY AND MANKIND,
WHO, OVERPLIED BY PVBLIC ENERGIES, DIED OF A NERVOVS FEVER,
IVLY VIIII, MDCCLXVI, AGED XXXXV

17. CIPRIANI, Giovanni Battista (1727-1785), Italian

Jonathan Mayhew (1720-1766), 1767

Etching. Plate mark: H. 24.2 x 18 cm.
Inscribed, within wreath: REMARKS / ON AN ANON. TRACT / P. LXXXII /
I AM INDEED / A / POOR / MAN; across lower portion of image:
IONATHON MAYHEW, D•D•PASTOR OF THE WEST CHVRCH / IN BOS-
TON, IN NEW ENGLAND, AN ASSERTOR OF THE CIVIL / AND RELIGIOVS
LIBERTIES OF HIS COVNTRY AND MANKIND, / WHO, OVERPLIED BY
PVBLIC ENERGIES, DIED OF A NERVOUS FEVER, / IVLY VIII, MDCCLVI,
AGED XXXXV; l.l: I•B•CIPRIANI; l.r. MDCCLXVII.
Fogg Art Museum, Print Department; gift of Mrs. Frederic T. Lewis,
in memory of Dr. Frederic T. Lewis (M 13,868)

Thomas Hollis V (cat. nos. 87-90) commissioned this etching of Rev. Jonathan Mayhew after the pastor's death. It is believed that the likeness — which Mrs. Mayhew thought the best portrait of her husband — was made from a crayon portrait drawn the day before Mayhew died.[1]

An Italian expatriate artist, Giovanni Battista Cipriani, engraved the portrait, but Thomas Hollis devised the symbols and inscription beneath the image. Two elaborate quill pens cross over a wreath that encloses a quotation and from which an archbishop's mitre hangs. The quotation is from *Remarks on an Anonymous Tract* (cat. no. 18), Mayhew's reply to the Archbishop of Canterbury, who had belittled Mayhew's apprehensions that an American episcopate might threaten colonial liberties as a "poor man's fears."

> I am indeed, even literally, a "poor man," as this gentleman calls me, I suppose, in another sense: . . . I had much rather be the *poor* son of a good man, who spent a long life and his patrimony in the humble and laborious, tho' apostolical employment of preaching the "unsearchable riches of Christ" to *poor Indians*; . . . than even the *rich* son and heir of One who had, by temporizing in religion, and tampering with politics, by flattering the Great, and prostituting his conscience, made his way to a bishoprick, and the worldly dignity of a peer; how large a *bag* soever

he had carried with him thro' a life of idleness and pride, of intrigue and luxury, or left behind him at death, the *black period* of all his greatness and glory.[2]

Beneath his own personal print of Mayhew, Hollis wrote these lines:

> The Serpent, Crosier-propt, high rear'd his head
> And through our World its poisnous Vapour Spread,
> Till Mayhew to the dust, the reptile frownd'd
> And from the Fangs took all their power to wound
> Now, Mitre-wreathed, upon the belly go
> And be hence forth to man, a harmless foe,
> To Modest worth thus Mitred pride gives way
> And Lambeth's self to Mayhew yields the day.[3]

G. B. Cipriani was born in Florence, where he received artistic training under Antonio Domenico Gabbiani and an Englishman, Hugford. He lived in Rome from 1750 until 1755, when his friends, Sir William Chambers (an architect) and Joseph Wilton (a sculptor), persuaded him to accompany them back to England. There he married a well-to-do Englishwoman and taught at the duke of Richmond's gallery. His reputation as a painter, engraver, and draftsman became widespread. Cipriani was one of the founding members of the Royal Academy, whose diploma and prize medals he designed, and where he often exhibited his works with another Italian, Bartolozzi, who made engravings after Cipriani's drawings and paintings.

His most important patron was probably Thomas Hollis (see cat. no. 87).

---

1. Akers, *Called Unto Liberty,* p. xii.
2. *Ibid.,* p. 193.
3. *Sibley's,* p. 460. Lambeth Palace is the official London residence of the Archbishop of Canterbury.

18. Mayhew, Jonathan

Remarks on an Anonymous Tract . . .

Boston: R. and S. Draper, 1764. H. 20.5 cm.
Lent by the Houghton Library; gift of John Holmes (*AC7.M4537.764r)

In this essay, his reply to a British pamphlet, Mayhew continued to regard Apthorp House as a signal that the Anglicans were preparing to establish an American bishopric:

> Let me add; since a mission was established at Cambridge, and a very sumptuous dwelling-house (for this country) erected there, that town hath been often talked of by episcopalians as well as others, as the proposed place of residence for a bishop; which I thought not improbable . . . (p. 58).

Referring to the threat to colonial liberties that the establishment of an American episcopate would present, Mayhew said,

> It is however, pretty evident from our history, that in arbitrary reigns, and foolish and wicked administrations, the bishops have commonly been *the most useful members, or instruments,* that the crown or court had, in establishing a tyranny over the bodies and souls of men, . . . The old cry, *No bishop, no King* has indeed been of mighty efficacy in times past (pp. 57-61).

58   A Second Defence of the Observations

First, he proposes that they fhould ' have no concern
' in the leaft with any *perfons* who do not profefs them-
' felves to be *of the church of England.*'‡

Secondly, he fays, ' it is not defired in the leaft that
' that they fhould hold courts to·try matrimonial or tefta-
' mentary caufes, or be vefted with any authority, now
' exercifed either by provincial governors or fubordinate
' magiftrates, or infringe or diminifh any *privileges* and
' *liberties* enjoyed by any of the laity,' &c. ‖ But that they
fhould be intirely confined to fuch *religious* and *facred offices
as the aforefaid.*

Thirdly, as to the place or places of the epifcopal refidence; he believes no *fingle perfon hath once named or
thought of* New-England, as a proper *place for the refidence
of a bifhop;* ' but *epifcopal colonies* have been always pro-
' pofed.'* And he thinks that fuch perfons fhould be fent
in this character, ' as are leaft likely to caufe *uneafinefs.*'§

This, he affures us, ' is the real and only fcheme that
' hath been planned for bifhops in America; and who-
· ever hath heard of any other, hath been mifinformed
' through miftake or defign.'†

To fpeak for my felf, then, I am one of thofe who have
been thus *mifinformed;* and I know of others who have
been fo, in common with me. I did not fuppofe, the *true*
fcheme was, that American bifhops fhould have *no* concern,
but with *epifcopalians;* or that they fhould be wholly confined to the *facred* offices aforefaid. As to the *place* of the
epifcopal refidence; I thought it not improbable, that if
feveral bifhops were fent, one of them would be ftationed
in *New-England*, to confirm and ordain; and to *blefs all
manner of people* here, *fufceptible*, &c. Let me add; fince a
miffion was eftablifhed at Cambridge, and a very fumptuous
dwelling-houfe (for this country) erected there, that town
hath been often talked of by epifcopalians as well as others,
as the propofed place of refidence for a bifhop; which I
thought not improbable. And I have reafon to take it a-
mifs that this gentleman, fpeaking of what I hinted about
Mr. *Apthorp*, and a *fuperb edifice in a neighbouring town*,
has

‡ P. 60.   ‖ Ibid.   * P. 66.   § P. 67.   † P. 60.

19. Political Register, vol. 5

London: Printed for Henry Beevor in Little-Britain, 1769. H. 21 cm.
Lent by Harvard College Library (BR 2062.16)

East Apthorp's return to England probably inspired this satirical print, *An Attempt to Land a Bishop in America.* It appeared in 1769 juxtaposed with "An Essay on Liberty and Independency," in the *Political Register,* a British periodical published by the radical printer John Almon who was a friend of Thomas Hollis.

The print shows a bishop, with crook and mitre below, who kneels praying, "Lord, now lettest thou thy Servant depart in Peace." He is on a ship, "The Hilsborough,"[1] which is being pushed off from the dock by two hearty colonists. Behind them stand a group of angry men, who are waving, and in some cases throwing, books by Locke, Sidney, Calvin, and Barclay. One man holds a banner which reads, "Liberty & Freedom of Conscience," while another is shouting, "No Lords Spiritual or Temporal in New England." A monkey sits in the foreground, near a paper which reads, "Shall they be obliged to maintain Bishops that cannot maintain themselves."

---

1. Lord Hillsborough was secretary of state for the colonies.

Design'd & Engrav'd for the Political Register.

An Attempt to land a Bishop in America.

20. COPLEY, John Singleton (1738-1815), American

Rev. Mather Byles (1707-1788), 1765-67

Oil on canvas. H. 76.8 x 64.3 cm.
Provenance: Descended through the Byles family to Mather Byles Des Brisay of Bridgewater, Nova Scotia; Frederick Lewis Gay (1908-23)
Lent by the American Antiquarian Society, Worcester, Massachusetts

The city's only *Tory* Congregational minister was the Rev. Mather Byles (A.B. 1725), the pastor of the Hollis Street Church and the grandson of Increase Mather. Although he tried not to mix politics and religion, his congregation did not approve of his relationship with the Loyalists and discharged him of his duties in 1776, after forty-three years as pastor. His name was added to the list of "enemies" to be deported, but he stayed in Boston, under house arrest, for two years.

Mather Byles was famous for his poetry, which ap-

peared in the *New-England Courant* and the *New-England Weekly Journal,* and for his puns. He called the armed guard stationed in front of his house his "observe-a-Tory." One day, he sent this guard on an errand, picked up his gun, and proceeded to march around in the guard's place. When the soldier returned, Byles declared that he had been "guarded, reguarded, and disreguarded."[1]

His grandson, the artist Mather Brown (see cat. no. 71), met John Singleton Copley, Benjamin West, and members of the British nobility through letters of introduction from the Reverend Dr. Byles and Byles' childhood friend, Benjamin Franklin. Franklin had recommended that the University of Aberdeen grant Byles a Doctor of Divinity degree in 1765 — in part out of gratitude for the Master of Arts degree that Harvard had awarded Franklin in 1753 on Byles' recommendation as an overseer of the College.

---

1. *Sibley's,* 7:486.

The Quincy Family

The Revolution divided some of Massachusetts' foremost families, among them the Quincys, whose story illustrates the unhappy predicament thrust upon some as tensions increased between Patriots and Loyalists.

By his first wife, Hannah Sturgis, Col. Josiah Quincy (cat. no 21) had four children: Edmund (A.B. 1752), who died at sea in 1768; Samuel (cat. no. 27); Hannah (cat. no. 29); and Josiah, Jr. (cat. no. 23). The two younger sons, Samuel and Josiah, were eminent lawyers in Boston. During the trial of the soldiers involved in the Boston Massacre, they were on opposite sides, with Josiah defending the soldiers, and Samuel — serving as solicitor general for the crown — prosecuting them. But the stands they took during the trial were a result of their professional commitments and not their personal principles. Later Josiah proved to be an ardent Patriot and Samuel, a Loyalist.

As the Revolution approached, Samuel Quincy wrote to his brother Josiah:

> The Convulsions of the times is in nothing more to be lamented, than the interruption of domestic Harmony. . . . Our natural Frame and Constitution, though cast in the same Mold, are not in all respects alike; nor is a difference in the turn of Mind, among branches of the same Family an uncommon appearance. . . . *Our* Notions both of Government and Religion may be variant, but perhaps are not altogether discordant. . . . I hope cannot fairly be imputed to Either of Us . . . a defect of Conscience or Uprightness of Intention.[1]

Josiah died at sea on 25 April 1775 while returning to his country from a mission to England he made on behalf of the Patriot cause. A little more than a week later, Samuel fled the colonies. The letters that Samuel sent from London to his wife, Hannah Hill Quincy (cat. no. 28), show the plight of the exiled Loyalist who had been separated from family and friends.

On New Year's Day, 1777, he wrote:

> The continuance of our unhappy separation has something in it so unexpected, so unprecedented, so complicated with evil, and misfortune, it has become almost too burdensome for my spirits,

nor have I words that can reach its description. I long much to see my father. It is now more than eighteen months since I parted with him in a manner I regret. Neither of you say anything of the family in Braintree. They ought not to think me regardess of them though I am silent; for, however lightly they may look upon me, I yet remember them with pleasure.[2]

And again, on 12 March 1777:

You inquire whether I cannot bear contempt and reproach, rather than remain any longer separated from my family? As I always wished, and I think always endeavored, not to deserve the one, so will I ever be careful to avoid the other. . . .

I am sorry you say nothing of my father, or the family at Braintree; I have not received a line or heard from them since I left America. . . . God bless you all; live happy, and think I am as much so as my long absence from you will permit.[3]

Samuel seemed to be particularly concerned with the grief he must have caused his father, whose favorite he had always been, and he continually tried to justify his decision to remain in England:

. . . It would grieve me very much to think of never again seeing my father, . . . but a return to my native country I cannot be reconciled to until I am convinced that I am as well thought of as I deserve to be. I shall ever rejoice in its prosperity, but am too proud to live despised where I was once respected — an object of insult instead of the child of favor.[4]

And, in 1779, before leaving for a new position in the West Indies, he wrote:

Transmit to my father every expression of duty and affection. If he retains the same friendship and parental fondness for me I have always experienced from him, he will patronize my children, and in doing this will do it unto me. It was my intention to have written to him, but the subjects of which I want to treat are too personally interesting for the casualties of the present day. He may rest assured it is my greatest unhappiness to be thus denied the pleasing task of lightening his misfortunes and soothing the evening of his days. . . .[5]

Josiah Quincy, Sr. did remember the children of his son, from whom he was separated by "the present unnatural war." He made special bequests to them upon his death.

---

1. *Sibley's,* 13:481-82. Samuel Quincy to Josiah Quincy, Jr., 1 June 1774. The original letter is in the Josiah Quincy, Jr. Papers, Massachusetts Historical Society, Boston.

2. James H. Stark, *The Loyalists of Massachusetts,* pp. 369-70. Samuel Quincy to Hannah Hill Quincy, 1 January 1777.

3. *Ibid.,* p. 370. Samuel Quincy to Hannah Hill Quincy, 12 March 1777.

4. *Ibid.,* p. 371. Samuel Quincy to Hannah Hill Quincy, 18 April 1778.

5. *Ibid.,* pp. 372-73. Samuel Quincy to Hannah Hill Quincy, 15 March 1779.

21. COPLEY, John Singleton (1738-1815), American

Josiah Quincy, Sr. (1709-1784), ca. 1767

Oil on canvas. H. 90.7 x 72 cm.
Provenance: Descendants of the subject; [Hirschl & Adler Galleries]
Lent by the Dietrich Brothers Americana Corporation, Philadelphia,
  Pennsylvania

Josiah Quincy, Sr. (A.B. 1728) was the son of Judge Edmund Quincy of Braintree and his wife Dorothy (Flynt) Quincy, sister of Harvard tutor Henry Flynt. In 1735 Quincy moved to Boston, where he became a partner in the mercantile firm of Quincy, Quincy, and Jackson. He was highly successful in business, and travelled often to Europe to secure supply contracts from both the French and the British.

In 1748 one of his ships captured a Spanish galleon carrying 161 chests of silver and gold. When the three partners divided the treasure, worth $300,000, Josiah was able to retire to Braintree. There he established a cider mill and a factory to manufacture spermaceti candles and glass, said to be the first glass works in America.

Quincy served on various town committees, in the House of Representatives, as justice of the peace, and as colonel of the Third Suffolk Regiment. In 1755 he and Thomas Pownall were sent by Governor Shirley to Pennsylvania to ask for aid in building a fort at Crown Point. Benjamin Franklin helped them raise £10,000 there.

After his second Braintree home burned in 1770, he built a new mansion with a view of Boston Harbor, from which he watched the movements of the British fleet and reported them to his friend George Washington. He scratched on one window pane, with his diamond ring: "Oct. 10, 1775, Governor Gage sailed for England with a fair wind."[1]

After the war, Col. Quincy resumed his duties as justice of the peace and continued his life as a country gentleman. It is said that he pursued his love of field sports until the last moment, dying as he sat on a block of ice on the beach, watching for wild ducks to fly overhead.

This elegant portrait of Quincy *père* shows us how the fashionable, wealthy merchant dressed in eighteenth-century Boston. Copley gave a great deal of attention to such details as the rococo lace cuffs, which can still be seen today at the Josiah Quincy Homestead in Wollaston, Massachusetts.

1. *Sibley's*, 8:473.

22. Quincy, Josiah, Sr.

Autograph letter, signed, to Benjamin Franklin. Braintree, 25 March 1775

Ink on cream antique laid paper. Folded, leaf: H. 22.5 x 18.5 cm.
Lent by the Massachusetts Historical Society, Boston

The correspondence between Colonel Quincy and Benjamin Franklin covered a variety of political and economic subjects. This particular letter discusses the Loyalist group to which Samuel Quincy belonged:

> You would hardly be persuaded to believe, did not melancholy Experience evince the Truth of it, that such a Number of infamous Wretches could be found upon the Continent, as are now group'd together in Boston, under the Pretence of flying thither from the Rage of popular Fury; when every Body knows, and their own Consciences cannot but dictate to them, that all they aim at, is, to recommend themselves to the first Offices of Trust and Power, in Case the Plan of subverting the present Constitution, and establishing a despotic Government in it's Stead, can be successfully carried into Execution.

23. STUART, Gilbert (1758-1828), American

Josiah Quincy, Jr. (1744-1775), 1825

Oil on canvas. H. 91.3 x 71.2 cm.
Provenance: Quincy Family
Lent by Edmund Quincy

Josiah Quincy, Jr., "the Patriot" (A.B. 1763), established a successful law practice after studying with Oxenbridge Thacher, a Whig attorney who had argued with James Otis against the writs of assistance.

By 1767 he was writing caustic articles in the *Boston Gazette,* criticizing the administration. Thus it was a surprise to many, most of all to his father, when Josiah agreed to represent the soldiers involved in the Boston Massacre on the grounds that they deserved an adequate defense. His position cost him many friends. The elder Quincy wrote to him:

> I am under great affliction at hearing the bitterest reproaches uttered against you, for having become an advocate for those criminals who are charged with the murder of their fellow-citizens. Good God! Is it possible? I will not believe it. . . .[1]

Josiah, Jr. remained active in the Whig cause: meeting with other members of the radical leadership in Boston, continuing to write vicious attacks on the administration under the pseudonyms "Marchmont Nedham" and "Needham's Remembrancer," corresponding with Whig leaders in other colonies, and publishing an influential pamphlet on the Boston Port Bill.

In the fall of 1774 he journeyed to England as the Patriots' "ambassador" to confer with the British Whigs and to check on Benjamin Franklin, whom Quincy had come to distrust. He met with the "friends of Liberty," with Franklin (whom he found to be loyal to the Patriot cause), and with various ministers of King George's government.

Frail and ill, but determined to return to America with secret information obtained in England, Quincy set sail in

March 1775. He died on 25 April 1775 off the coast of Gloucester. He was buried at Gloucester, but after the siege of Boston, his body was removed to Braintree.

Gilbert Stuart painted this half-length portrait of Josiah Quincy in his graduating gown fifty years after the subject's death, in October-November 1825. The artist used both a description of Quincy provided by his widow and a statuette of John Wilkes. Josiah resembled Wilkes in looks as well as principles, and he was often mistaken for him while in London.[2]

Gilbert Stuart grew up in Rhode Island, the son of a Scottish snuff-grinder. After studying with Cosmo Alexander, who had taken him to Edinburgh, Stuart began painting the portraits of prominent Newport families.

The Revolution soon interrupted his business. Since most of his family and clients were in sympathy with the crown, Stuart decided to leave the colonies. His boat left Boston on the day before the battle of Bunker Hill, the last such vessel to clear that port.

In London, Stuart assisted and studied with a fellow American artist, Benjamin West, a court painter to King George III. After five years, young Stuart was able to open his own studio, and by 1784 his fame as a portrait painter was well established.

An invitation by the duke of Rutland — and possibly a desire to escape the high debts caused by an extravagant life style — prompted the Stuart family to move to Ireland in 1787. Although the painter had many commissions there, his debts continued to mount.

Early in 1793 he left for America with the scheme of making a fortune by painting George Washington's portrait. Stuart was the social rage in New York and subsequently in Philadelphia, the seat of the federal government, where he finally had the opportunity to paint the president's likeness. Indeed, it is through Stuart's "Athenaeum" portrait — the model for the Washington on stamps and one dollar bills — that our first president is known to most of us.

When the capital moved to Washington, D.C., in 1803, Gilbert Stuart moved with it to paint Thomas Jefferson and James Madison. In 1805 Stuart came to Boston, where he continued to paint portraits of the leading people of his time until his death in 1828.

---

1. *Sibley's,* 8:471.
2. This information was given to me by Edmund Quincy, in his letter of 3 March 1975. For political reasons, Thomas Hutchinson called Josiah Quincy, Jr. "Wilkes Quincy."

24. Quincy, Josiah, Sr.

Autograph letter, signed, to Josiah Quincy, Jr. n.p., 26 November 1774

Ink on cream antique laid paper. Folded, leaf: H. 23.5 x 19 cm.
Lent by the Massachusetts Historical Society, Boston

The letter was written on the eve of Josiah Quincy, Jr.'s mission to England. His father told him that "all of the Tories & some of the Whigs resent your clandestine Departure: Many of The Former say, that as soon as your Arrival is known you will be apprehended and secured...."

Colonel Quincy reported to his son the various speculations surrounding this trip: rumors of his going to Holland, or to the South of France, for his health and other reasons.

Thus, you see, how much you are a gen[l]: Subject of Conversation: Perhaps there never was an American, not even a D[ickinson] nor a F[ranklin], whose Abilities have raised the Expectations of their American Brethren more than yours: God Almighty grant, if your Life and Health is spared, that you may exceed them in every Respect.

money too much, to be hushed at a Court where every thing is bought & sold:

That, they could not refute your Arguments, in Defence of your Country,

they would offer invincible Arguments to induce you to betray it.

Thus you see, how much you are a gen.l Subject of Conversation: Perhaps, there

never was an American, not even a D——— nor a F———, whose Abilities have raised,

The Expectations of their american Brethren more ~than yours~ God Almighty grant! if —

your Life and Health is spared, that you may exceed them in every Respect.

~I had the Pleasure~ last Monday, ~I~ dined with your Wife at her

Father's where I had the Pleasure of seeing & caressing both my dear grand Children

the lovely Beuy & his Mamma, I expect, the Week after next, will come & spend a

Month or two with us: When in Town, I found ~two~ political Productions: —

An Essay on the Constitution; Power of G.t Britain over the Colonies in America &c.:

and a Letter from L.d Lyttelton to L.d Chatham on the Quebec Bill: They are

each of them ~both~ esteem'd masterly Performances, by their respective Partizans:

Before this reaches you, I doubt not you will have rec.d the Former from its Author,

whose distinguished Abilities shine thro' this, equally, if not superior to his former

Productions: however I regret his allowing g.t Britain a Revenue from the Colonies,

whilst ~she~ persists in her Claim of an exclusive Trade with them; which appears

to me to be, an over Ballance for all the Protection She has, or can afford us.

especially when it is considered, that all the Profits resulting from the immense

Extent of Territory, ceded to her at the Treaty of Paris, remain solely to her, at the

same Time we are restrained from the ~profitable~ whale & cod Fishery in the Bay of S.t Lawrence

& Straights of Belisle which we formerly enjoyed without Interruption: But perhaps

I am mistaken & therefore submit to his better Judgment.

If I am not greatly mistaken, there is not a single Argum.t

in L.d Lyttelton's L.r whereby he endeavours to prove the ~future~ Wisdom Benevolence and

Policy of Parliament in indulging the Canadeans with the french Laws

~which~ won't much more forceably conclude in ~favour~ ^Behalf of these Colonies that

Their respective Constitutions & Laws sh.d remain inviolate & the Rights

& Privileges secured by them upon no Pretence whatever ~be~ abridged:

where then is the wisdom, the Benevolence & Justice of Parliament; and

what

25. Quincy, Josiah, Jr.

Journal of London Mission, 1774-75

Ink on paper. H. 16.5 x 10 cm.
Lent by the Massachusetts Historical Society, Boston

The journal records Quincy's voyage from Salem to Cornwall and, in almost daily entries, provides us with an account of his activities in England from November 1774 until March 1775.

Quincy spent a great deal of time with Franklin and other "friends of Liberty," discussing the current situation in America and the next course of action that New England, in particular, ought to pursue. He also met with Lords North and Dartmouth and attended sessions of the House of Commons and the House of Lords, where he was moved to hear William Pitt, earl of Chatham, deliver a strong appeal on behalf of the American cause.

His health grew worse in January, but by the end of the following month, he had made plans to return to his native country:

It is a good deal against my own private opinion and inclination that I now sail for America. . . . On the other hand, my most intimate friends (except for Mr. Bromfield) insist upon my going directly to Boston: they say no letters can go with safety; and that I can deliver more information and advice viva voce than could or ought to be wrote. They say my going now must be (if I arrive safely) of great advantage to the American Cause.[1]

1. This journal has been printed in the *Proceedings of the Massachusetts Historical Society*, 50:433-96.

26. Quincy, Josiah, Jr.

Manuscript copy of his Will. 20 February 1774

Ink on cream paper. H. 31.5 x 19.5 cm.
Lent by the Massachusetts Historical Society, Boston

> . . . I give to my son Josiah when he shall arive to the Age of Fifteen Years Algernon Sidneys works . . ., John Lockes Works . . ., Lord Bacons works . . ., Gordons Tacitus . . ., Gordons Sallust, Cato's Letters by Gordon & Trenchard & Mrs MCauleys History of England. May the Spirit of Liberty rest upon him. . . .

With these few volumes, Josiah, Jr. tried to transmit the radical Whig tradition to his son, Josiah III, then only three years of age, later a Federalist congressman, mayor of Boston, and president of Harvard.

Greek and Roman authors, such as Plutarch, Cicero, Sallust, and Tacitus, were often quoted in the literature of the American Revolution. The colonists saw a close connection between these writers' essays on the decadence of Rome, for example, and their concern with the threatened corruption of their own liberties and virtues.[1] Other writers from other times further influenced their attitudes and ideas, among them the Enlightenment rationalist, John Locke (see cat. no. 93). But the most important source of revolutionary thought came from the writers of the English Civil War and the period of the Commonwealth. John Milton (see cat. no. 95), Algernon Sidney (see cat. no. 94), John Trenchard, and Thomas Gordon brought all the other streams of thought into a coherent whole.[2]

---

1. Bailyn, *Ideological Origins*, pp. 23-66.
2. *Ibid.*, pp. 34-36.

27. COPLEY, John Singleton (1738-1815), American

Samuel Quincy (1734-1789), ca. 1767

Oil on canvas. H. 90.2 x 71.7 cm.
Provenance: Quincy Phillips, great-grandson of the sitter, Cambridge, Massachusetts, by 1873; Emily Treadwell Phillips, his wife; Grace Treadwell, her niece, Kittery Point, Maine
Lent by Museum of Fine Arts, Boston; bequest of Miss Grace W. Treadwell (1970.356)

Josiah Quincy's second son, Samuel (A.B. 1754), was thought at first to sympathize with the Sons of Liberty and the Whig cause. But by 1774 he had signed the farewell address to Gov. Thomas Hutchinson, and on 13 May 1775, as he made plans to leave America, he wrote to his brother-in-law Henry Hill:

> I am going, my dear friend, to quit the habitation where I have been so long encircled with the dearest connections.
>
> I am going to hazard the unstable element, and for a while to change the scene — whether it will be prosperous or adverse, is not for me to determine. . . . My political character with you may be suspicious; but be assured, if I cannot *serve* my country, which I shall endeavor to the utmost of my power, I will never *betray* it.[1]

Samuel Quincy departed from Marblehead aboard the ship *Minerva* on 27 May 1775, never again to see New England. The former solicitor general did not intend to be away more than a few months, but events did not come about in the way he had imagined. He was banished from Massachusetts, for having "joined the enemy," in 1778, and his property was confiscated and sold at auction in 1779. This was something he could not understand.

> The Love of one's country, and solicitude for its welfare, are natural and laudable affections; to lose its good opinion is at once unhappy, and attended with many ill consequences; how much more unfortunate to be forever excluded from it without offence![2]

While Quincy first enjoyed his stay in England — sightseeing, theatre-going, meeting with other Loyalists — he soon found it difficult to be without family, friends, or employment. He decided that his best prospects for fortune lay in Antigua and was finally able to procure the position of comptroller of customs for the Port of Parham in 1779. His law practice in the West Indies allowed him to live quite comfortably there.

Quincy became ill on a voyage to England in 1789 and died within sight of Bristol, where he was buried.

This portrait by Copley was executed about the same time as the portrait of Samuel's father, Josiah Quincy, Sr. (cat. no. 21), and the two paintings are similar in composition, with the head off-center to the left of the canvas.

---

1. Stark, *Loyalists of Massachusetts,* pp. 368-69.
2. *Ibid.,* p. 371. Samuel Quincy to Hannah Hill Quincy, 31 May 1778.

28. COPLEY, John Singleton (1738-1815), American

Hannah Hill Quincy (Mrs. Samuel Quincy, 1734-1782), ca. 1761

Oil on canvas. H. 90.2 x 71.7 cm.
Provenance: Quincy Phillips, great-grandson of the sitter, Cambridge, Massachusetts, by 1873; Emily Treadwell Phillips, his wife; Grace Treadwell, her niece, Kittery Point, Maine
Lent by the Museum of Fine Arts, Boston; bequest of Mrs. Grace W. Treadwell (1970.357)

Hannah Hill, daughter of a Boston distiller, married Samuel Quincy in 1761, probably the year that this portrait was painted by Copley. They lived in Boston until 1775, when Samuel booked passage for England, and she chose to go to Cambridge to live with her brother, Henry Hill, a Patriot.

In a letter, written 15 October 1777, Samuel advises his "Sophia":

> If things should not wear a more promising aspect at the opening of the next year, by all means summon resolution to cross the ocean. But if there is an appearance of accommodating this truly unnatural contest, it would be advisable for you to bear farther promise; as I mean to return to my native country whenever I may be permitted, and there is a chance for my procuring a livelihood. . . .[1]

In a later letter written from London, 18 April 1778, he explains to her that he cannot return until "I am convinced that I am as well thought of as I know I deserve to be."[2]

Although most sources state that Hannah Quincy died without seeing her husband again, Clifford Shipton disagrees. Shipton believes that Samuel Quincy sent for his wife, who came to Antigua with two of their children, Hannah and Tom (young Sam was at Harvard), and that she died there in November 1782.[3]

Jules Prown suggests that this elegant portrait derives its pose from Rubens' portrait of *Helena Fourment,* used by

many mid-eighteenth century English painters in several variations.[4]

---

1. Stark, *Loyalists of Massachusetts*, p. 370.   3. *Sibley's*, 13:486.
2. *Ibid.*, p. 371.

29. Derived from an unknown original

Hannah Quincy Lincoln Storer (Mrs. Ebenezer Storer, 1736-1826)

Pastel and watercolor over photograph. Image: Oval H. 17.4 X 13 cm.; sheet: H. 23.1 X 20 cm.
Provenance: Francis Storer Eaton, great-grandson of the sitter
Harvard University Portrait Collection; gift of Francis Storer Eaton (H 559)

As a young girl in Braintree, Hannah Quincy had many suitors, including John Adams. In 1759 Hannah was often mentioned in his diary as "O" which stood for the whimsical name of Orlinda. He was impressed by her lively intellect and high principles.

In 1760, however, Hannah married a Hingham doctor, Bela Lincoln (A.B. 1754), whose father, like hers, was a distinguished colonel in the Suffolk Regiment. Their unhappy marriage ended with Lincoln's death in 1774, and Hannah returned to her father's house where she lived until she married Ebenezer Storer (cat. no. 51) in 1777.[1] There she witnessed the elder Quincy's anguish at seeing his only living son turn against his native country. On 11 May 1775 she wrote to her brother Samuel, who was preparing to leave with other exiles:

> Let it not be told in America, and let it not be published in Great Britain, that a brother of such brothers fled from his country — the wife of his youth — the children of his affection — and from his aged sire, already bowed down with the loss of two sons, and by that of many more dear, though not so near connection, to secure himself from the reproaches of his injured countrymen, and to cover such a retreat, obliged to enlist as a sycophant under an obnoxious Hutchinson, who is a tool under a cruel North, and by them to be veered about, and at last to be blown aside with a cool "tomorrow, sir."[2]

The portraits of Hannah and Ebenezer Storer came to Harvard as works by Skipworth, dated ca. 1804. But when the miniatures were recently examined in the Fogg's conservation laboratory, it seemed possible that they might be nineteenth-century photographs reworked with chalks and watercolor. A corner of the heavy cardstock, on which both were drawn, was taken from the portrait of Mrs. Storer, and a half-dozen samples, taken from various layers, were subjected to emission spectrographic analysis. A significant amount of silver and a smaller amount of gold were detected in the front surface only of the cardstock. This indicated that it had been coated with photosensitive chemicals.

1. I am indebted to Dr. Zoltan Haraszti for allowing me to see parts of his manuscript for a book about John Adams as a young man.
2. George Atkinson Ward, *Journal and Letters of Samuel Curwen*, p. 563.

Hutchinson-Oliver Letters

In 1772 Benjamin Franklin (cat. no. 34), the colonial agent for the Massachusetts House, obtained ten letters, written between 1767 and 1769 by Thomas Hutchinson (cat. no. 30), Andrew Oliver, Sr. (cat. no. 31), and several other Massachusetts officials to Thomas Whately.[1] Whately, who died in 1772, had been a member of Parliament and secretary to the treasury in Grenville's ministry. With access to high authorities, he could easily pass on to the administration the reports, opinions, and requests of the colonists who wrote to him.

Hutchinson's letters described the radical proceedings of the Massachusetts Assembly, the "licentiousness" of the Sons of Liberty, and the scandalous essays printed in the Boston newspapers. One letter (see cat. no. 32) mentioned the inevitability of "an abridgement of what are called English liberties" for the colonies due to the distance separating them from England. Andrew Oliver, in his correspondence, sought a position for his son Daniel, increased salaries for the governor, lieutenant governor, and judges, and a legislative council composed of an "order of Patricians," men possessing "landed estate of one hundred pounds per year."

The letters, culled from a much larger group, were assembled in 1770 to support a proposal then under consideration by a parliamentary committee to change the Massachusetts Charter. Although it is not certain, the best evidence indicates that Thomas Pownall (member of Parliament and former governor of Massachusetts) was the one who passed the letters on to Franklin.[2] As Franklin later explained in his "Tract Relative to the Affair of Hutchinson's Letters," they were offered as proof from a "Gentleman of Character and Distinction" that the recent despised measures (including the sending of troops to Boston) did not come from the British government, "but were projected, proposed to Administration, solicited, and obtained by some of the most respectable among the Americans themselves, as necessary Measures for the welfare of that Country."[3]

Hoping to reconcile the colonists and their mother country — and perhaps also believing that he needed to remove doubts about his reliability as a Patriot advocate — Franklin borrowed the letters and sent them on 2 December 1772 to Thomas Cushing, Speaker of the Massachusetts House of Representatives. Because of conditions attached to the loan, Franklin instructed Cushing to show the letters only to the Committee of Correspondence, to "Messrs. Bowdoin and Pitts of the Council, and Drs. Chauncey, and Winthrop, with a few such other Gentlemen as you may think fit to show them to."[4] The correspondence was not to be copied or published.

Opposition to the restrictions mounted immediately. John Adams showed the letters to Patriots along his superior court circuit, and Sam Adams read them aloud to the House. In mid-June, Sam Adams announced that copies of the correspondence had been received from a source other than the original one and were circulating in Boston. Cushing and the other recipients thereupon decided to permit publication. The Boston Committee of Correspondence sent copies to other towns in Massachusetts together with a statement (cat. no. 33) saying that God had intended to make the letters public.

While Franklin may have hoped that knowledge of the letters would lead to reconciliation by directing the suspicions of the colonists away from the ministry, the result was just the opposite. Publication of the correspondence convinced "untold thousands of Americans that all the rumors of plots against their liberties were true and that hopes of reconciliation were unrealistic."[5] Franklin was right, however, in thinking that his countrymen would direct their immediate rage at the letters' authors, especially Thomas Hutchinson. The Massachusetts governor was burned in effigy in Philadelphia and Princeton. John Adams, writing as "Novanglus" cursed this "vile serpent...bone of our bone, born and educated among us." The Massachusetts House of Representatives sent a petition to King George III demanding the recall of both Hutchinson and Oliver, and passed, by large majority, a set of resolutions attacking their governor and lieutenant governor. The letters, said the resolutions,

> had a natural and *efficacious* tendency to interrupt and alienate the affections of our most gracious sovereign King George the Third, from this his loyal and affectionate province; to destroy that harmony and good-will between Great Britain and this colony, which every friend to either would wish to establish; to excite the resentment of the British administration against this province; to

defeat the endeavours of our agents and friends to serve us by a fair representation of our state of grievances; to prevent our humble and repeated petitions from reaching the royal ear of our common sovereign; and *to produce the severe and destructive measures,* which have been taken against this province, and others more so, which have been threatened. . . .[6]

Hutchinson and Oliver's effectiveness had been irreparably damaged. Ironically, in the case of Hutchinson at least, the letters contained nothing he had not said before in public. As published, however, they not only put the governor in the worst possible light, but actually misrepresented his beliefs.

Franklin's policy of reconciliation failed, but his standing among the American Patriots, often shaky, was now secure. In London, he had been vilified in the press and censured and ridiculed by the solicitor general, Alexander Wedderburn (cat. no. 35), before the Privy Council at Whitehall. Wedderburn, pounding the table, directed invectives at Franklin for nearly an hour. He said that "no gentleman's papers would now be safe unless locked into his escretoire. . . . Franklin will henceforth esteem it a libel to be called a man of letters. . . . I hope, my Lords, you will mark and brand this man. . . . He has forfeited all the respect of societies of men. Into what companies will he hereafter go with an unembarrassed face of the honest intrepidity of virtue?"[7]

---

1. The other correspondents were Hutchinson's nephew, Nathaniel Rogers, Hutchinson's friend and protégé, Charles Paxton, and Tory attorney Robert Auchmuty.

2. Bernard Bailyn, *Ordeal of Thomas Hutchinson,* pp. 229-36.

3. Benjamin Franklin, "Tract Relating to the Affair of Hutchinson's Letters," p. 262.

4. *Ibid.,* pp. 266-67.

5. Bailyn, *Ordeal,* pp. 224-25.

6. Franklin, "Tract," p. 277.

7. Catherine Drinker Bowen, *Most Dangerous Man in America,* pp. 236, 240.

30. TRUMAN, Edward (active 1741), English

Thomas Hutchinson (1711-1780), 1741

Oil on canvas. H. 69.1 x 57.8 cm.
Lent by the Massachusetts Historical Society, Boston

Thomas Hutchinson (A.B. 1727) entered his father's countinghouse after graduating from Harvard. A shrewd businessman, he was successful enough by 1742 to purchase ninety-five acres in Milton overlooking Boston Harbor as a site for the elegant mansion that he liked to call his "Cottage in the Country."[1]

Following Hutchinson's appointment as chief justice in 1760, his two older sons, Thomas, Jr. and Elisha, took over most of the family business, and he devoted himself to public life. He had previously held the posts of selectman, representative, Speaker of the House, president of the Council, judge of probate, and justice of common pleas for Suffolk. After 1760 he served first as lieutenant governor, then as acting governor until, in 1771, he was appointed governor. Unquestionably one of the most influential men in Massachusetts politics, he came to be one of the most mistrusted as well because of the large number of offices that he and his family held.

Ironically, however, Hutchinson was ambivalent about accepting the public positions that brought him most of his troubles: the chief justiceship and the governorship. Lacking any formal legal training, he agreed to serve as chief justice only when Governor Bernard seemed to allow him no alternative; and he was so unsure of his abilities to act as governor that at one point he withdrew his name from consideration for the job.

But perhaps the greatest irony of Hutchinson's career was that he opposed the very measures that were so unpopular in the colonies. He worked to avert the Stamp Act, for instance. But he never questioned Parliament's authority to impose such a measure, and his countrymen suspected him of secretly favoring the Act. Thus it was

that on 26 August 1765 a mob "more violent . . . than any that would be seen in the entire course of the Revolution" plundered his Boston house.[2] While the family fled into the streets, rioters axed down the doors, tore up the furnishings, and looted money, silver, clothing, books, and papers.

Two years later, in 1767, the Townshend Duties brought further upheaval. Viewing the turmoil around him, Hutchinson harkened back to the days of his ancestor Anne Hutchinson, the religious radical who had been exiled from Massachusetts: "the frenzy was not higher," he wrote, "when they banished my pious great grandmother."[3] Subject to unremitting pressure, uncertain of his abilities, and painfully sensitive to the opprobrium heaped upon him, Hutchinson apparently suffered a nervous breakdown.[4]

Yet the worst was still to come. In 1773, Hutchinson was crushingly reprimanded by his superiors for entering into a debate with the Massachusetts Assembly concerning Parliament's authority over the colonies. Hard on the heels of that humiliation came the publication of the Hutchinson-Oliver Letters (cat. no. 32), followed in December by the final crisis: the Boston Tea Party.

Hoping to be relieved of his office, Hutchinson had to endure a further six months of vilification, until General Gage's arrival in June 1774 as military governor allowed him to sail for England. Hutchinson was warmly received in London, but he never adjusted to his exile and longed constantly for Massachusetts.

In 1777, he wrote to his cousin, Edward Hutchinson, explaining his last wish:

> to convince my countrymen of one truth (which I feel the force of to my own great comfort every day) that I never, in my public character, took one step in which I did not mean to serve their true interest, and to preserve to them every liberty consistent with it, or with their connection with the kingdom. Whether they, or I, mistook their true interest, time will discover.[5]

Although he always hoped to lay his "bones in New England," even this was denied him. He died in England on 5 June 1780 and was buried at Croydon.

This portrait of young Thomas Hutchinson was painted by Edward Truman, a little-known English artist. It was executed in 1741 while Hutchinson was in England, as agent for the province, seeking audiences with the Privy Council and Board of Trade concerning some border disputes with New Hampshire.[6] The painting was badly damaged in the Stamp Act riots of 1765.

1. Bailyn, *Ordeal of Thomas Hutchinson*, p. 39. Upon his father's death in 1739, Thomas inherited the family mansion on Garden Court Street.
2. *Ibid.*, p. 35.
3. *Ibid.*, p. 138
4. *Ibid.*, p. 139.
5. *Ibid.*, p. 372.
6. Malcolm Freiberg, "Thomas Hutchinson," p. 43.

31. EMMONS, Nathaniel (1704-1740), American

Lt. Gov. Andrew Oliver (1706-1774), 1728

Oil on wood panel. H. 36.8 x 25.5 cm. Signed and dated, l.r.:
  NEmmons Pinxt Dec[r] 1728
Provenance: Grace Lyde Gordon, descendant of the subject by his
  second wife; William H. P. Oliver (1920-1950); Andrew Oliver
  (1950)
Lent by the Oliver Family

Although Andrew Oliver (A.B. 1724) was a successful
Boston merchant, his public career occupied most of his
time and energy. He was a generous benefactor of Harvard, donating books and manuscripts, and an active supporter of Old South Church and the Society for Promoting
the Gospel in New England. In his long career, he served
as justice of the peace, member of the House of Representatives and the Council, and secretary of the province.

In 1765 Andrew Oliver was appointed stamp agent,
and his popularity immediately collapsed. His effigy was
hung and burned on 14 August of that year, his warehouse
was sacked and his mansion vandalized, with Oliver
barely escaping the rioters. Mobs continued to harass the
Oliver family until 17 December 1765 when two thousand
persons witnessed the stamp distributor's resignation under the Liberty Tree.

He was not re-elected to the Council in 1766, but was
sworn in as lieutenant governor in 1771, upon Thomas
Hutchinson's appointment as governor. In 1773, with the
publication of the Hutchinson-Oliver Letters, his political
career was brought to an end.

Andrew Oliver, Sr. died in 1774. Once a popular leader
of Massachusetts, his funeral was more like that of a trai-
tor or an enemy. His brother Peter was even afraid to attend. Cheering mobs followed the funeral procession and
several nearby towns flew flags to celebrate his death.

There are five extant works by Nathaniel Emmons, Boston landscape and portrait painter. One is this signed and

dated portrait of the young merchant Andrew Oliver. Typical of Emmons' style, it resembles a portrait engraving, with its small size, black and white tonality, and added inscription. Several scholars have noted the artist's reliance on English engravings, and one has traced the source of the Oliver portrait to Kneller's mezzotint of Charles Montagu.[1]

Emmons was a popular figure in early eighteenth-century Boston, as his obituary in the *New England Journal* (27 May 1740) attests:

> He was universally own'd to be the greatest master of various sorts of painting that ever was born in this Country. And his excellent Works were the pure effect of his own Genius, without receiving any Instructions from others. . . . He was sober and modest; minded accuracy more than Profit.[2]

---

1. Charles Coleman Sellers, "Mezzotint Prototypes of Colonial Portraiture," pp. 421-22.
2. George Francis Dow, *The Arts and Crafts in New England 1704-1775*, p. 2.

32. Copy of the Letters Sent to Great-Britain, by his Excellency Thomas Hutchinson, The Hon. Andrew Oliver, and Several Other Persons, Born and Educated Among Us

Boston: Edes and Gill, 1773. H. 20.5 cm., irregular
Lent by the Houghton Library (*AC7.H9748.773c)

This excerpt from a letter to Thomas Whately, written by Thomas Hutchinson on 20 January 1769, destroyed Hutchinson's political effectiveness in America.

> I never think of the measures necessary for the peace and good order of the colonies without pain. There must be an abridgment of what are called English liberties. I relieve myself by considering that in a remove from the state of nature to the most perfect state of government there must be a great restraint of natural liberty. I doubt whether it is possible to project a system of government in which a colony 3000 miles distant from the parent state shall enjoy all the liberty of the parent state. I am certain I have never yet seen the projection. I wish the good of the colony when I wish to see some further restraint of liberty rather than the connexion with the parent state should be broken; for I am sure such a breach must prove the ruin of the colony (p. 16).

The title page of this volume states that the book is one in which "the judicious Reader will discover the fatal Source of the Confusion and Bloodshed in which this Province especially has been involved, and which threatned total Destruction to the Liberties of all *America*" (p. 1).

33. Boston Committee of Correspondence

Circular Letter, 22 June 1773

Printed on cream antique laid paper. H. 27 x 18 cm.
By courtesy of the Trustees of the Boston Public Library (xbH.90A.38)

The Boston Committee of Correspondence distributed the Hutchinson-Oliver Letters and the House of Representatives' set of resolutions with this printed letter in the summer of 1773. Signed by William Cooper, town clerk of Boston, the document told of the plot laid by "our malicious and insidious Enemies." The letter cited the resolves, which reported that Governor Hutchinson

> has been exerting himself . . . by his secret confidential Correspondence, to introduce Measures destructive of our constitutional Liberty, while he has practiced every method among the People of this Province, to fix in their Minds an exalted Opinion of his warmest Affection for them, and his unremitted Endeavors to promote their best Interest at the Court of Great-Britain.

The Committee called for the "strictest Concurrence in Sentiment and Action of every individual of this Province, and . . . of THIS CONTINENT; 'By uniting we stand,' and shall be able to defeat the Invaders and Violaters of our Rights."

C O P Y

OF

L E T T E R S

Sent to *Great-Britain*, by his Excellency *Thomas Hutchinson*, the Hon. *Andrew Oliver*, and several other Persons, BORN AND EDUCATED AMONG US.

Which original Letters have been returned to *America*, and laid before the honorable House of Representatives of this Province.

In which (*notwithstanding his Excellency's Declaration to the House, that the Tendency and Design of them was not to subvert the Constitution, but rather to preserve it entire*) the judicious Reader will discover the fatal Source of the Confusion and Bloodshed in which this Province especially has been involved, and which threatned total Destruction to the Liberties of all *America*.

B O S T O N:

Printed by EDES and GILL, in Queen-Street; 1773.

32

33H.90a.38

BOSTON, JUNE 22d, 1773.

SIR,

THE Committee of Correspondence of the Town of *Boston*, conformable to that Duty which they have hitherto endeavoured to discharge with Fidelity, again address you with a very fortunate important Discovery ; and cannot but express their grateful Sentiments in having obtained the Approbation of so large a Majority of the Towns in this Colony, for their past Attention to the general Interest.

A more extraordinary Occurrence possibly never yet took Place in *America*; the Providential Care of that gracious Being who conducted the early Settlers of this Country to establish a safe Retreat from Tyranny for themselves and their Posterity in *America*, has again wonderfully interposed to bring to Light the Plot that had been laid for us by our malicious and insidious Enemies.

Our present Governor has been exerting himself (as the honorable House of Assembly have expressed themselves in their late Resolves) " by his secret confidential Correspondence, to introduce Measures " destructive of our constitutional Liberty, while he has practiced every " method among the People of this Province, to fix in their Minds " an exalted Opinion of his warmest Affection for them, and his " unremitted Endeavours to promote their best Interest at the Court " of Great-Britain." This will abundantly appear by the Letters and Resolves which we herewith transmit to you; the serious Perusal of which will shew you your present most dangerous Situation. This Period calls for the strictest Concurrence in Sentiment and Action of every individual of this Province, and we may add, of THIS CONTINENT; all private Views should be annihilated, and the Good of the Whole should be the single Object of our Pursuit— " By uniting we stand," and shall be able to defeat the Invaders and Violaters of our Rights.

We are,

Your Friends and humble Servants,

Signed by Direction of the Committee for Correspondence in *Boston,*

William Cooper } *Town-Clerk.*

To the Town-Clerk of   , to be immediately delivered to the Committee of Correspondence for your Town, if such a Committee is chosen, otherwise to the Gentlemen the Selectmen, to be communicated to the Town.

c

33

B. Franklin of Philadelphia L.L.D. F.R.S.

34. FISHER, Edward (1730-1785), English, after Mason Chamberlin (d. 1787), English

Benjamin Franklin, 1763

Mezzotint (second state) on cream antique laid paper; plate re-touched with burin. Cut to plate mark: H. 37.6 x 27.5 cm.

Inscribed, below design area, l.l: M:Chamberlin pinx.; l.r.: E. Fisher fecit,; l.c.: B. Franklin of Philadelphia L.L.D. F.R.S./Sold by M.. Chamberlin in Stewart Street, Old Artillery Ground, Spittalfields,— Price 5″

Provenance: Harvard College Archives (1771-1944)

Fogg Art Museum, Print Department; gift of Benjamin Franklin, 1771 (M10,977)

Benjamin Franklin (honorary A.M. 1753) was born in Boston, the son of an immigrant English soap and candle maker. After about a year's formal education, he worked briefly with his father and then served an unhappy apprenticeship with his older brother James, a printer.

Eventually, young Franklin established his own printing business in Philadelphia, where he bought a newspaper, *The Pennsylvania Gazette,* which enabled him to publicize his causes and projects. Among the many organizations he helped to found were the Library Company of Philadelphia, the Union Fire Company, the American Philosophical Society, the Academy of Philadelphia (now called the University of Pennsylvania), and the Pennsylvania Hospital.

He also found time to experiment with electricity and to correspond with scientists in the colonies and the mother country. His "great Improvements in Philosophic Learning, & particularly wth. Respect to Electricity," led the President and Fellows of Harvard College to bestow on Franklin the degree of Master of Arts in 1753. This was Franklin's first academic degree, and is usually counted the first honorary A.M. degree awarded by Harvard.

Franklin had been and continued to be a generous supporter of Harvard, even though at a precocious sixteen years of age, he had written (under the name of Silence

Dogood) a satirical article on the College in his brother's paper, *The New-England Courant*. As a colonial agent in London (first for Pennsylvania, then for Georgia, New Jersey, and the Massachusetts House of Representatives), he also served informally as an agent for Harvard. He procured the finest books and scientific instruments to replace those lost in the 1764 fire. He also sent several personal gifts, including a plaster bust of the colonies' champion, William Pitt, earl of Chatham, and this Edward Fisher mezzotint.

Franklin's tenure in London came to an end with the publication of the Hutchinson-Oliver Letters and his subsequent censure by Alexander Wedderburn (cat. no. 35). He was summarily dismissed as deputy postmaster general of America, a position he had held since 1753.

After his return to Philadelphia in 1775, he was immediately elected postmaster general and sent to the Second Continental Congress, then in session in that city. Because of his many European friends, he was selected as one of three commissioners sent to France in 1776 to negotiate for alliance and assistance. Aid finally came in 1779, largely due to the efforts of Franklin, who was named minister plenipotentiary to the Court of France. In 1781 he was appointed a peace commissioner. And, in 1783, Franklin, who had signed the Declaration of Independence, placed his signature on the peace treaty with England.

This portrait is taken from the painting (now in the Philadelphia Museum of Art) which Col. Philip Ludwell III, a well-to-do Virginian living in England, commissioned Mason Chamberlin to execute in 1762. Franklin posed for the portrait just before he left for Philadelphia in late July or early August of that year. It depicts him seated inside, while a thunderstorm outside enables him to observe the phenomena of electricity and lightning. Franklin was very pleased with this painting and he ordered a replica, which he presented to his son William, governor of New Jersey.

William Franklin had already ordered a hundred mezzotints of this portrait. They were made in 1763 by Edward Fisher, an Irishman who lived in Leicester Square and engraved works after Chamberlin, Wilson, and Reynolds.[1] William's father likewise ordered a large quantity of prints, presenting them to John Winthrop, Mather Byles, and Harvard College, among others. Charles Sellers has pointed out that Franklin freely sent such mementos to his friends, with whom he could not visit. Franklin enclosed one of the Fisher mezzotints in a letter to Thomas François Dalibard, saying "As I cannot soon again enjoy the Happiness of being personally in your Company, permit my Shadow to pay my Respects to you...."[2] And again, in a letter to Jonathan Williams, Sr., he mentioned the prints: "I have taken a Dozen of them to send to Boston & it being the only way in which I am now likely to visit my Friends there, I hope a long Visit in this shape will not be disagreeable to them."[3]

---

1. John Chaloner Smith, *British Mezzotint Portraits*, 2:485-86.
2. Charles Coleman Sellers, *Benjamin Franklin in Portraiture*, p. 221. Benjamin Franklin to Thomas François Dalibard, 22 September 1769.
3. *Ibid.*, p. 57. Benjamin Franklin to Jonathan Williams, Sr., 24 February 1764.

35. ORME, Daniel (ca. 1766-ca. 1832), English

Alexander Wedderburn (1733-1805), First Baron Lough-
borough (in 1780) and First Earl of Rosslyn (1801),
1796

Engraving. Image: H. 16 x 10.5 cm.; sheet: H. 23 x 29 cm.
Inscribed, within oval: Orme Junᴿ Sculptᵗ; l.c.: Lord Loughborough/
Published July 1, 1796 by J. Sewell, Cornhill, London.
Provenance: Mellen Chamberlain Autograph Collection
By courtesy of the Trustees of the Boston Public Library; from the
Mellen Chamberlain Autograph Collection (CH.G.7.11)

In 1771, after switching parties several times, Alexander
Wedderburn returned to the Tories for good when Lord
North offered him the position of solicitor general and
membership in the Privy Council. It was before North's
Council that Wedderburn strongly censured Benjamin
Franklin in 1774.

A favorite of George III's friend and adviser, Lord Bute,
the ambitious Wedderburn enjoyed a soaring career,
accepting one position after another: attorney general
(1778); chief justice of common pleas (1780-93); and lord
chancellor (1793-1801).

Daniel Orme was portrait painter and engraver to King
George III. He exhibited at the Royal Academy from 1797
until 1801.

Interrelation of Families

The politics of eighteenth-century Massachusetts to a considerable extent were the politics of influence and family. The Otises, the Adamses, and the Bowdoin-Temple-Erving clan were foremost among powerful family alliances on the Patriot side that sought as much as anything else to advance the interests of their members.

But the most striking colonial family network was that of the Hutchinsons and Olivers, leaders of the Loyalists. United by multiple marriages over two generations, these families enjoyed an unparalleled dominance in Massachusetts politics for almost twenty years. Andrew Oliver and Thomas Hutchinson married sisters, and four children from their unions intermarried, cementing an alliance that was feared and envied by its rivals. The political consequences were formidable:

> Andrew Oliver's brother Peter — brother, that is of the lieutenant governor and father-in-law of one of the governor's children — had been associate justice of the superior court since 1756, and became chief justice when Hutchinson resigned that post to assume the governorship. Thus, all of the three Hutchinson children who married, married Olivers, and they did so during the first three years of Hutchinson's governorship. And thus, too, three brothers and brothers-in-law occupied simultaneously in the 1770's the governorship, the lieutenant governorship, and the chief justice-ship of Massachusetts. No one but a Hutchinson or an Oliver had been lieutenant governor of Massachusetts after 1758 or chief justice after 1760.[1]

These were only the salient features of the alliance. On a somewhat lesser level, the governor's brother, Foster Hutchinson, was an associate justice of the Superior Court, while a nephew, Nathaniel Rogers, became province secretary succeeding Andrew Oliver. Another nephew, Samuel Mather, was a customs clerk, and a brother-in-law, John Cotton, held a post in the Vice Admirality Court. By marriage, the Olivers were related to other important New England families, among them the Lyndes and the Clarkes (see cat. nos. 40-42).

Ironically, the very alliance that gave the Hutchinsons and Olivers enormous power to reward friends and punish opponents also made them fatally vulnerable by isolating them from their fellow colonists. As tensions mounted, Governor Hutchinson looked increasingly to his family for support, and finding there a mirror for his own beliefs and prejudices, he never grasped the nature of the changes that were transforming Massachusetts.

1. Bailyn, *Ordeal of Thomas Hutchinson*, p. 31.

Chart I: Interrelation of Families

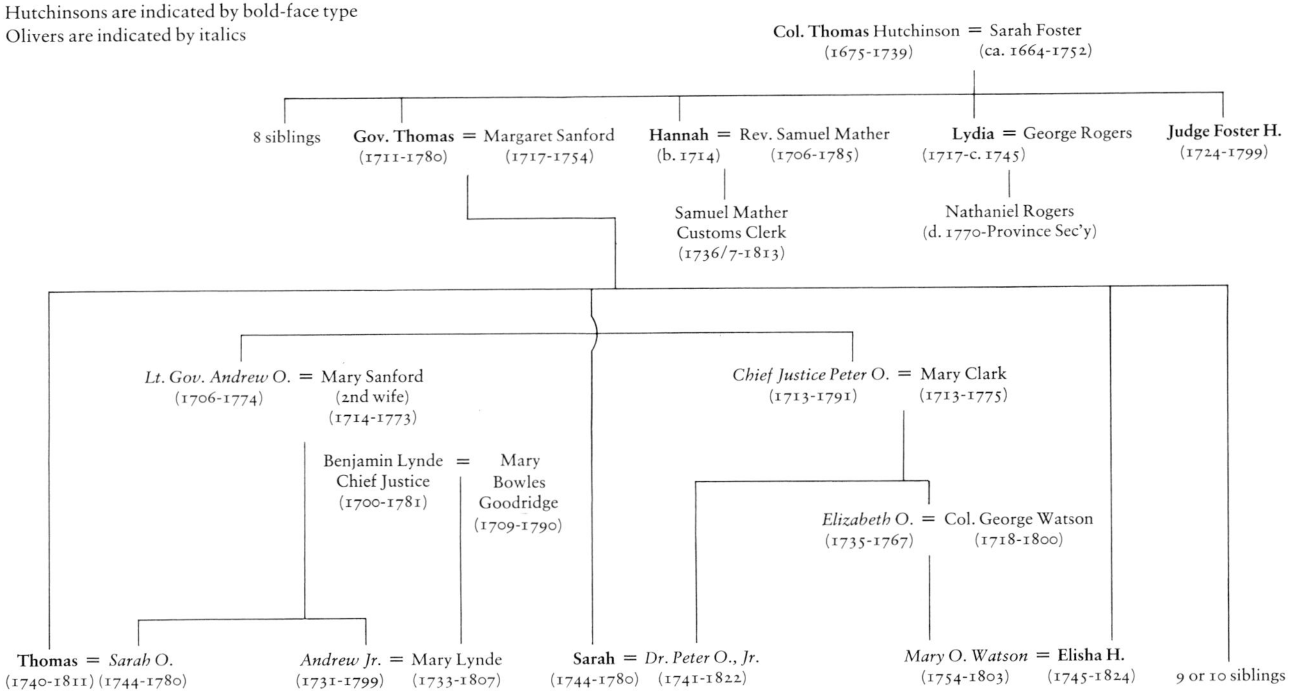

Hutchinsons are indicated by bold-face type
Olivers are indicated by italics

36. COPLEY, John Singleton (1738-1815), American

Mary Sanford Oliver (Mrs. Andrew Oliver, Sr., 1714-1773), ca. 1758

Oil on copper. H. 4.5 x 3.7 cm.
Provenance: John Marshall Phillips (1952-55)
Lent by Yale University Art Gallery; Mabel Brady Garvan Fund (1955.5.12)

On Monday, 23 December 1734, the *New England Weekly Journal* announced that

> On Thursday evening last Mr. Andrew Oliver Merchant of this Place, and Nephew to his Excellency our Governor, was married to Mrs. Mary Sanford, a young Lady of desirable Accomplishments, and a plentiful Fortune.[1]

Mary Sanford, whose sister Margaret was the wife of Thomas Hutchinson was Andrew Oliver's second wife. He had lost his first wife, Mary Fitch, in 1732, after only four years of marriage.

Copley painted portraits of many of the residents of Boston's South End between 1758 and 1761, including two pairs of miniatures of Mr. and Mrs. Andrew Oliver, Sr. Miniatures such as this one were highly popular during the period and were considered family heirlooms.

---

1. *New England Weekly Journal,* 23 December 1734, p. 2. This is on microfilm at Lamont Library, Harvard.

37. BLACKBURN, Joseph (fl. 1752-1763), English

Hon. Andrew Oliver, Jr. (1731-1799), 1755

Oil on canvas. H. 127 x 101.7 cm. Signed and dated, l.l.: I Blackburn
Pinx 1755
Provenance: Hon. Andrew Oliver, Jr. (1755-ca. 1799); B. Lynde
Oliver, Salem (ca. 1799-1835); B. Lynde Oliver, his nephew (1835-
1843); listed in his inventory by Mr. Briggs, his administrator and
brother-in-law (1843); Sarah Pynchon Oliver, Lynde's sister (1844);
Rev. Andrew Oliver, her nephew (1844-1898); William H. P.
Oliver, his son (1898-1950); Andrew Oliver, his son (1950)
Lent by the Oliver Family

Andrew Oliver, Jr. (A.B. 1749) was the second son of Lt.
Gov. Andrew and Mary (Fitch) Oliver. After his Boston
home was burned in the fire of 1760, Oliver moved to
Salem, where he joined various clubs, was appointed judge
of the Court of Common Pleas for Essex County (1761)
and elected to the House of Representatives (1762).

Rather than politics, it seems he preferred the study of
"natural philosophy," corresponding with leading scientists such as Herschel and Winthrop, and writing papers
on such phenomena as comets, lightning, and water-
spouts. He was a founder and fellow of the American
Academy of Arts and Sciences and a member of the American Philosophical Society.

As political tensions increased, however, unruly mobs
disrupted the peace of Salem, and Oliver travelled the
countryside, staying in small villages. When he arrived in
Boston in 1774, he was surprised to find that he had been
named a mandamus councillor. He resigned the office
after ten days and returned to Salem, where he remained
for the rest of his life. He was the only member of his family not forced into exile.

In 1795, Andrew wrote to Daniel Oliver, a relative in
exile:

> This country is advancing to dignity and opulence with
> an accelerated velocity. You would be much surprised
> could you see the improvement in the capital. . . . The

present destracted state of Europe, affords a very strong contrast to the tranquil and flourishing state of this country.[1]

Joseph Blackburn, a British portraitist, was working in Bermuda by 1753. He went to Rhode Island in 1754, and then to Boston in 1755 where he remained (with a few trips to Portsmouth, New Hampshire) until 1763.

Blackburn's English rococo style greatly appealed to New England's leading families, who liked to keep up with London's fashions. The Olivers, Apthorps, Bowdoins, Faneuils, and Bulfinches flocked to him with portrait commissions. They delighted in his elegant and sophisticated handling of fabrics — delicate laces and shiny satins — and jewels, and his graceful handling of the figure.[2] These characteristics can clearly be seen in the companion portrait of Mrs. Andrew Oliver, Jr. (cat. no. 38).

Blackburn cannot be traced beyond 1763, but his influence remained in Boston and can be seen in the elegant portraits painted by John Singleton Copley about 1756/57.[3]

---

1. *Sibley's,* 12:460-61. Andrew Oliver to Daniel Oliver, 7 July 1795.
2. Lawrence Park, "Joseph Blackburn," p. 277.
3. Jules David Prown, *John Singleton Copley,* 1:22.

38

38. BLACKBURN, Joseph (fl. 1752-1763), English

Mary Lynde Oliver (Mrs. Andrew Oliver, Jr., 1733-1807), 1755

Oil on canvas. H. 127 x 101.7 cm. Signed and dated, l.l.: I Blackburn
   Pinx 1755
Provenance: Hon. Andrew Oliver, Jr. (1755-ca. 1799); B. Lynde
   Oliver, Salem (ca. 1799-1835); B. Lynde Oliver, his nephew (1835-
   1843); listed in his inventory by Mr. Briggs, his administrator and
   brother-in-law (1843); Sarah Pynchon Oliver, Lynde's sister (1844);
   Rev. Andrew Oliver, her nephew (1844-1898); William H. P. Oli-
   ver, his son (1898-1950); Andrew Oliver, his son (1950)
Lent by the Oliver Family

Mary Lynde, eldest daughter of the Honorable and Mrs.
Benjamin Lynde, Jr. (cat. nos. 40, 41) of Salem, married
Andrew Oliver, Jr. in 1752. After the war, the Olivers

moved to the Lynde mansion in Salem, where the "most
learned men of the town" enjoyed conversation, the harp-
sichord, and tea.

Rev. William Bentley, the Salem diarist, described Mrs.
Andrew Oliver, Jr. in her later years as a lady "of real
piety, but not of that mind which could have rendered her
a fit companion for her husband who took a high rank in
American Literature. She was feeble limited in her en-
quiries, & a century too late in her manners."[1]

1. Park, "Joseph Blackburn," p. 307.

39. Boston, 18th century

Double Chairback Settee, 1770-80

Mahogany with maple and pine. H. 95.2, W. 160, D. 55.2 cm.
Provenance: Melvill(e) Family
Anonymous Loan

This rare Chippendale settee (which has two matching
side chairs) was probably made around 1774, the year that
its owner, Thomas Melvill (see cat. no. 3) married Priscilla Scollay, daughter of a wealthy Boston merchant.
Melvill, an ardent Patriot, joined the Continental Army
when the fighting began, serving as captain and then as
major in an artillery regiment. After the war, he served as
a naval officer for the port of Boston and, from 1779 until
1825, as fireward in that town. In honor of his command
of a group of volunteer fire companies, one of the fire en-
gines was named "Melvill." He was remembered for being the last man in Boston to wear the cocked hat and
knee breeches, the costume of the revolutionary era.[1] It
is also said that he was the subject of Oliver Wendell
Holmes, Sr.'s poem "The Last Leaf."[2] At the age of eighty-
one he died of over-exertion at a fire near his home.

1. Francis S. Drake, ed., *Tea Leaves,* p. 135.
2. Henry Wilder Foote, "Benjamin Blyth of Salem," p. 96.

40. Attributed to SMIBERT, John (1688-1751), Scottish

Benjamin Lynde, Jr. (1700-1781), ca. 1738

Oil on canvas. H. 70.5 x 62.9 cm.
Provenance: Lynde Family; Oliver Family; Dr. Fitch E. Oliver, Boston; Mrs. F. E. Oliver; Mr. Frederick Strong Moseley, Boston (ca. 1910); Mrs. F. S. Moseley
Lent by Frederick Strong Moseley III

The Honorable Benjamin Lynde, Jr. (A.B. 1718) was the eldest son of Benjamin and Mary (Browne) Lynde of Salem. Young Lynde, a merchant and lawyer, was active as treasurer for the town of Salem; he served as its delegate to the House of Representatives and held appointments on the Court of Common Pleas and the Superior Court. He became well known in 1770 when he was given the responsibility of presiding over the Boston Massacre trial. In 1771 he succeeded Thomas Hutchinson as chief justice, a post which the elder Lynde had earlier held. He resigned in less than a year, over a controversy concerning the payment of judges' salaries, and was appointed to the Essex probate court.

Benjamin Lynde, Jr. seemed to have moderate Loyalist sympathies, with friends and family on the Tory side. In 1775, he moved to Ipswich Hamlet (now Hamilton), where he remained for the next eighteen months. He was back in Salem, however, for the winter of 1776/77. He died in Danvers at the age of eighty-one.

This painting has traditionally been attributed to John Smibert, who worked in Boston from 1720 until his death in 1751.[1] Smibert was not only a prolific portraitist, but also the architect who designed Faneuil Hall. His house became the art center for the colonies. There he sold art supplies and prints and exhibited his own works as well as copies of paintings and sculpture from Italy.

Although Smibert's *Notebook*[2] records a portrait of "Judge Lynds" in June 1737, this most likely refers to the portrait of Judge Benjamin Lynde, Sr. (1666-1745; A.B.

1686), Benjamin Jr.'s father. This portrait of the younger Lynde resembles that of his father, but does not have the vitality and superior technique demonstrated in the former work.[3]

1. Alan Burroughs has attributed this portrait to John Smibert's son Nathaniel (1734-1756) in "Paintings by Nathaniel Smibert," *Art in America*, 31:88-97.
2. The *Notebook* was recently discovered in London's Public Record Office and then published in facsimile by the Massachusetts Historical Society. It includes dates of Smibert's move from Edinburgh to London (1709), his trip to Italy (1719-1722), and his journey to America (1728-1729). (He was to be professor of art and architecture at Dean Berkeley's proposed college in Bermuda.) In the *Notebook*, Smibert recorded his London (1722-1728) and American (1729-1746) portraits, with names of sitters, dates, sizes, and prices.
3. Henry Wilder Foote, *John Smibert, Painter*, pp. 219-20.

41. FEKE, Robert (fl. 1741-1750), American

Mary Bowles Goodridge Lynde (Mrs. Benjamin Lynde, Jr., 1709-1790), ca. 1748

Oil on canvas. H. 73.5 x 62.7 cm.
Provenance: Lynde family; Oliver family; Dr. Fitch E. Oliver, Boston; Mrs. F. E. Oliver; Mr. Frederick Strong Moseley, Boston (ca. 1910); Mrs. F. S. Moseley
Lent by Frederick Strong Moseley III

Mary Bowles Goodridge, widow of Capt. Walter Goodridge, married Benjamin Lynde, Jr. on 1 November 1731. Family tradition attributed this portrait to Smibert, but Henry Wilder Foote identified it as "one of the best of Feke's portraits of women," and dated it ca. 1748.[1] Although Mary Lynde lived in Salem, she may have sat for the portrait while travelling with her husband on court business, or visiting her father, John Bowles, who lived in Roxbury.

America's first major native artist, Robert Feke was born ca. 1707 in Oyster Bay, Long Island. Although he settled

40

41

in Newport, he visited New York, Philadelphia, and Boston from time to time in order to paint the portraits of the leading families in those cities.

On Feke's first trip to Boston in 1741, he looked for inspiration to John Smibert, who was the most gifted artist in the city and whose works he could study there. Feke's *Isaac Royall and Family* (owned by the Harvard Law School) is clearly modeled on Smibert's *Bermuda Group*. But by the time Robert Feke returned to Boston in 1748, he was so well-known that he did not even have to advertise his visit.[2] He went back to Newport for a year, following the successful Boston tour (he had painted over twenty portraits there in 1748), and then journeyed to Philadelphia. None of his portraits post-date 1750, and his whereabouts are unknown after 1751. It is thought that, due to ill health, he left for the warmer climate of Bermuda or Barbados, where he probably died.[3]

1. Henry Wilder Foote, *Robert Feke,* p. 163.
2. *Ibid.,* p. 75.
3. Peter Mooz, "Colonial Art" in *The Genius of American Painting,* p. 60.

42. COPLEY, John Singleton (1738-1815), American

Sketch for **The Copley Family,** 1776

Oil on canvas. H. 52.1 x 66.6 cm.
Provenance: Greene and Amory families
Anonymous Loan

John Singleton Copley was probably born in Boston to
Irish immigrant parents. After his father's death, Copley's
mother married the artist and teacher Peter Pelham, and
it was from Pelham that the young Copley probably received his only artistic training. Pelham died in 1751, and
within two years John Copley, still only in his mid-teens,
was engraving and painting to help support his family.

He rose to the pinnacle of the Boston art world, painting portraits of the city's elite and their wives. He painted
over 275 of them, both Patriots and Loyalists: merchants,
landed gentry, clergymen, and lawyers. Bostonians valued
his paintings for their realism, elegance, and sophistication.

His social and financial position increased with the
commissions. In 1767 he was able to write that he made
"as much as if I were a Raphael or Correggio." He married Susanna "Sukey" Clarke in 1769. They lived on a
twenty-acre estate on Beacon Hill, near John Hancock.

Benjamin West, with whom Copley had been corresponding, persistently advised the young artist to study
the Old Masters of Europe. Copley heeded this advice in
1774. His decision to leave the colonies was probably
hastened by the increasing tension in Boston between
Patriots and Loyalists. Jules Prown notes that the artist's
patronage was decreasing due to the political turmoil and
that the clients who remained were ordering smaller portraits, which brought him less money.[1]

Copley had tried to remain non-partisan, believing, as
he wrote Benjamin West on 24 November 1770, that politics was "neighther pleasing to an artist or advantageous
to the Art itself." But neutrality was more difficult to
maintain when his father-in-law, Richard Clarke, a Tory

and nephew of Gov. Thomas Hutchinson, became the target of mob attacks.

Clarke (A.B. 1729) was a prominent social and financial figure in pre-revolutionary Boston. He had a large importing business with his sons, Isaac and Jonathan, and in 1773 he became the main consignee for the taxed tea. Then and there his problems began. His mansion and warehouse were vandalized when he refused to resign as tea agent, and he and the other consignees soon took refuge at Castle William. Although John Copley tried to negotiate with the angry townspeople on behalf of his father-in-law, they were not appeased. On 16 December 1773 the Sons of Liberty, in three hours, emptied 342 chests of tea worth £18,000 into Boston Harbor.

Six months later, Copley set sail for England. From there, he journeyed first to France and then to Italy, where he wrote to Henry Pelham on 14 March 1775:

> could anything be more fortunate than the time of my leaving Boston? poor America! I hope the best but I fear the worst. Yet certain I am She will finally Imerge from he[r] present Callamity and become a Mighty Empire.[2]

"Sukey" had remained in Boston, but in May 1775, she, too, left with her three oldest children (the baby being too ill to travel). The family was reunited in London in the fall of 1775, when Copley returned from Italy. Richard Clarke soon joined them there.

They first settled in Leicester Square, the art center of London, but moved in 1783 to a more fashionable home in Hanover Square. Clarke and, to a lesser extent, Copley moved in the Tory circles of London society (especially among the Hutchinsons), meeting for weekly dinners with other New England expatriates at the Adelphi Club.

John Singleton Copley continued his successful career in England, where he was elected to the Royal Academy in 1776. His portraits were still in demand, although he increasingly became involved in history painting, which brought him great fame.

He was paralyzed by a stroke in August 1815 and died later that year. He was buried in the Hutchinson tomb in Croydon, England.

This painting, the sketch for a larger work in the National Gallery of Art, Washington, D.C., depicts the artist and his family shortly after their reunion in England. In addition to "Sukey" and Richard Clarke, there are four children represented: Elizabeth, who later married Gardiner Greene of Boston; Mary; John Jr., who became Lord Lyndhurst, lord chancellor of England; and the infant Clarke, who had been too frail to leave Boston and died there in 1776.[3]

---

1. Prown, *John Singleton Copley*, 1:86.
2. *Letters and Papers of John Singleton Copley and Henry Pelham, 1739-1776*, p. 301.
3. Prown (*Copley*, 2:262) notes that in the finished version, the baby is Susanna, born in England in 1776.

III. Harvard in the Revolutionary Era

In 1768 a group of discontented Harvard students gathered under the "Liberty Tree" (opposite Hollis Hall) to protest against a College rule they thought "unconstitutional." That same year students supported the non-importation agreements, voting to abstain from tea, to have their degrees printed on American paper, and to wear homespun suits to commencement. In 1769 they met in Holden Chapel where the General Court was sitting, and listened to the fiery orations of James Otis, Jr. "The young gentlemen are already taken up with politics," wrote Rev. Andrew Eliot to Thomas Hollis in 1770. "They have caught the spirit of the times. Their declamations and forensic disputes breathe the spirit of liberty."[1] Indeed, the topics brought before the Speaking Club focused on oppression and tyranny, while Harvard's military company, the Marti-Mercurian Band, drilled in the Yard.

Although the students followed one tradition in 1771 by holding a ceremony to welcome the new governor, Thomas Hutchinson, they broke with another that same year when, instead of having the Tory *Boston News-Letter* print their commencement theses, they gave the job to a Patriot paper, Isaiah Thomas's *Massachusetts Spy*.

On 18 July 1774 the Harvard Corporation chose a new president at Treasurer John Hancock's Beacon Hill mansion.[2] He was Samuel Langdon (A.B. 1740), a minister and secretary of the Sons of Liberty in Portsmouth, New Hampshire. Langdon was installed secretly on 14 October, the usual ceremonies seeming "altogether inexpedient," since the Corporation was trying to exclude Governor Gage and his mandamus councillors, who were *ex officio* members of the Board of Overseers.

There were a few Loyalists at Harvard, however. It has been calculated that sixteen per cent of the Harvard graduates alive on 1 January 1776 were Loyalists.[3] A band of Tory undergraduates incited a minor riot when, on 1 March 1775, they brought the forbidden tea into the College Commons. Patriot students rallied to defend their cause of the day, but in April, not more than six students joined the Minutemen at Lexington and Concord.

On 1 May 1775 the Massachusetts Committee of Safety ordered Harvard's students to leave Cambridge. The Provincial Congress commandeered the College buildings for quartering the American soldiers and on 15 June voted that the library and scientific apparatus be transported to Andover. The Board of Overseers met with Corporation representatives John Winthrop (cat. no. 98) and Samuel Cooper (cat. no. 8) to determine where the College should convene that fall. They considered Andover, Haverhill, Worcester, and Northampton before finally recommending that the students reassemble on 4 October 1775 in Concord, "where all necessary provision is made for their reception & they will have boarding & Chamber furniture at a reasonable Rate, & . . . the Presidents, Professors & Tutors will attend to the usual Business & Instruction of the College."[4]

Many students, however, did not go to Concord. Only twenty-four freshmen entered, and it has been estimated that not more than 100 students in all attended Harvard that year.[5] They lodged in homes (and some in taverns) throughout the town, as did the president and faculty, who brought along the College's clock, fire engine, museum, and scientific instruments in December (the library had been in Concord since October).

Classes were held in the town's meetinghouse, courthouse, and schoolhouse. And because of the scattering of students and professors — some were two miles outside of Concord — only two recitations per day were required.[6] Winter vacation was extended that year, although the students had not received a fall vacation and would not receive one the following spring.

On 3 April 1776 the President and Fellows met in Watertown and voted to confer the LL.D. degree on George Washington (see cat. nos. 44, 45). They also sought reimbursement from the Continental Congress for the damages to the College buildings by the American troops.

The students, many of whom had been living in unsatisfactory rooms (some unheated), were growing restless. In May they asked to be allowed to return to Cambridge. The President and Fellows presented their request to the General Court, and on 11 June 1776, Harvard College was given permission to return home. The following day, President Langdon thanked the townspeople of Concord for the friendship and accommodation, adding: "We hope the scholars while here have not dishonored themselves and the society by any incivilities or indecencies of behavior, or that you will readily forgive any errors which may be attributed to the inadvertence of youth."[7] By 21 June 1776, Harvard was back in Cambridge.

There was no public commencement that year (there were none between 1774 and 1781), but the graduates received a general diploma, containing forty-three names, signed by the members of the Harvard Corporation.

In October and November of 1777 the College feared it might have to give up its buildings once again, this time to Gen. John Burgoyne's surrendered soldiers (see "Cambridge During the Revolutionary Era"). But Harvard stubbornly — and successfully — held onto its quarters.

The College's problems only increased as the War for Independence continued. Its buildings were wrecked by the soldiers' occupation; each year saw fewer students, soaring inflation, and a constant shortage of books and supplies. There was no tea, coffee, or chocolate, and little salt. Breakfast and supper consisted of little more than a pint of milk and a biscuit. Pots, pans, plates, spoons, and other utensils had been taken by the soldiers. President Langdon wrote to his friend at Yale, Pres. Ezra Stiles: "When will our vile Currency come to its desired End? . . . We have once more tho't it necessary to pass the Commencement in Silence; near half the Senior Class impoverish'd by the Depreciation of the Currency. . . ."[8]

Harvard was not even sure how much money it had, since Treasurer Hancock repeatedly refused to settle accounts (see cat. no. 49). In 1777 Ebenezer Storer (cat. no. 51) was chosen to replace Hancock. A shrewd investor, Storer was able to triple the College's holdings by 1793. Harvard's economic health was further improved as wealthy businessmen such as James Bowdoin and John Lowell replaced professors, tutors, and clergymen as members of the Corporation.[9]

The College faced its last crisis of the revolutionary era in 1780 when student pressure led to the resignation of Pres. Samuel Langdon. An undergraduate committee addressed him in this way: "As a man of genius and knowledge we respect you; as a man of piety and virtue we venerate you; as a President we despise you."[10] Langdon, who had led Harvard College through some of its most difficult years, left Cambridge and accepted an appointment as preacher in Hampton Falls, New Hampshire, where he lived until his death.

---

1. Samuel Eliot Morison, *Three Centuries of Harvard, 1636-1936*, p. 138.
2. Hancock had been named treasurer of the College in 1773 (see cat. no. 49).
3. Morison, *Three Centuries*, p. 147n.
4. Percy Brown, "The Sojourn of Harvard College in Concord," p. 499.
5. Morison, *Three Centuries*, p. 149; Brown, "Sojourn," p. 499.
6. Brown, "Sojourn," p. 500.
7. *Ibid.*, p. 507.
8. *Sibley's*, 10:519. Samuel Langdon to Ezra Stiles, 26 June 1780.
9. Morison, *Three Centuries*, pp. 157-58.
10. *Sibley's*, 10:521.

43. Wadsworth House, November 1975

Photograph. H. 28 x 35 cm.
Paul Birnbaum, photographer

Benjamin Wadsworth (A.B. 1690) was installed as president of Harvard College on 7 July 1725. About six months later, the Massachusetts General Court voted

> that the Sum of One Thousand Pounds be allowed and paid out of the Public Treasury to the Corporation of *Harvard College*, . . . for the Building and Finishing a handsome Wooden Dwelling House, Barn, Out-Housen, &c. on some part of the Lands Adjacent and belonging to the said College, which is for the Reception and

Accommodation of the Reverend the President of *Harvard College,* for the time being.[1]

This fourth presidential mansion actually cost £1800, although the General Court would not increase its appropriation. The Early Georgian building was raised on 24 May 1726 and, even though the interior was not yet finished, President and Mrs. Wadsworth moved in on 4 November of that year.

In the 1760s Massachusetts Avenue east of Harvard Square was only a lane, called The Way to the Parsonage. Wadsworth House faced this, with a large front garden. Part of the College Yard was used for the president's orchard (fertilized from the "south privy") and his stable. Across the street was a lot where he could grow hay or other crops.[2]

On 26 June 1775 the Provincial Congress ordered that, except for one room reserved for Pres. Samuel Langdon, Wadsworth House be "cleared, prepared, and furnished, for the reception of the Commander-in-Chief and General Lee."[3] The house served as Washington's headquarters for the following two or three weeks. During the siege of Boston, it was used for the commissary department.

Two bays were added in 1783 to enlarge the house and, in 1810, another wooden addition was built at the rear of the house.

Wadsworth House, one of the few large houses in Cambridge not built for a Tory, served as Harvard's presidential residence for over a century. After Edward Everett's tenure ended in 1849, it was used for a myriad of purposes: boarding-house, dormitory, printing office, hygiene department, residence for visiting preachers, personnel relations, among others. Today it serves as the university marshal's office and alumni office, as well as headquarters for *Harvard Magazine.*

1. Hamilton Vaughan Bail, *Views of Harvard,* p. 68.
2. Morison, *Three Centuries,* pp. 77-78.
3. *Sibley's,* 12:501.

44. SAVAGE, Edward (1761-1817), American

George Washington (1732-1799), 1790

Oil on canvas. H. 74.8 x 62 cm. Signed and dated, l.l.: E. Savage
Pinx / 1790.
Harvard University Portrait Collection; gift of Edward Savage, 1791
(H 49)

On 2 July 1775 Harvard's president, Samuel Langdon,
welcomed George Washington (honorary LL.D. 1776)
into his home. The following day, tradition tells us, Washington took command of the Continental Army under a
large elm tree on Cambridge Common.

Later in July, he made plans to move into the fine house
of Maj. John Vassall, a Tory who had fled to Boston a few
months earlier. Perhaps this house, with its view of the
river, reminded him of Mount Vernon. Vassall's house
had been recently occupied by troops from Marblehead,
and Washington personally paid to have it put in good
order. There he (and later Mrs. Washington) remained
until the British evacuation of 1776.

The next time Washington visited Cambridge, he was
president of the United States. He came in October 1789,
accompanied by Vice Pres. John Adams and James Bowdoin. Pres. Joseph Willard personally gave them a tour
of the College, showing off the library, museum, and
scientific instruments.

Washington had no direct contact with Harvard after
this, although he did recommend it to parents with sons of
college age because the students were "less prone to dissi-
pation and debauchery than they are at the Colleges South
of it."[1]

In 1789 Edward Savage offered to paint George Washington's portrait for Harvard College. President Willard
wrote a letter of introduction which Savage carried to
Washington in New York, saying that

it would be exceedingly grateful to all the governors of
this literary society, that the portrait of the man we so

highly love, esteem, and revere, should be the property of and placed within Harvard College. . . .[2]

Washington replied the following month:

> Your letter of the 7th Ultimo was handed to me a few days since by Mr. Savage, who is now engaged in taking the Portrait which you, and the Governors of the Seminary over which you preside, have expressed a desire for, that it may be placed in the Philosophy Chamber of your University. I am induced, sir, to comply with this request from a wish that I have to gratify, so far as with propriety may be done, every reasonable desire of the Patrons and promoters of Science. And at the same time I feel myself flattered by the polite manner in which I am requested and good wishes for the prosperity of the University of Cambridge.[3]

Apparently, the sittings for the portrait took three days. On 21 December 1789 Washington wrote in his diary: "Sat from ten to one o'clock for a Mr. Savage, to draw my portrait for the University in Cambridge, in the State of Massachusetts, at the request of the President and Governors of the said University." Another entry on 28 December 1789 stated: "Sat all the forenoon for Mr. Savage who is taking my portrait." The last sitting occurred on 6 January 1790: "Sat from half after eight o'clock until ten for the portrait painter Mr. Savage, to finish the picture of me which he had begun for the University of Cambridge."[4]

Savage gave the portrait to Harvard and, on 30 August 1791, the Corporation thanked him and hung it in the Philosophy Chamber. The portrait depicts Washington in his continental uniform with the Order of the Cincinnati eagle in his left lapel.

Edward Savage, who was born in Princeton, Massachusetts, was trained as a goldsmith. But by his mid-twenties, he was painting copies after Copley, and after completing Washington's portrait, he went to Europe, where he studied under Benjamin West.

Working in Boston and later in Philadelphia, he became a well-known engraver. He successively opened galleries in Philadelphia (1796), New York (1802), and Boston (1812), where his work was displayed. His last years were spent on his farm in Princeton, where he died in 1817.

1. *Sibley's*, 12:506.
2. Louisa Dresser, "Edward Savage, Painter 1761-1817," p. 193. Joseph Willard to George Washington, 7 November 1789.
3. *Ibid.*, George Washington to Joseph Willard, 23 December 1789.
4. *Ibid.*, Washington's diary.

45. Langdon, Samuel (1722/3-1802)

Doctor of Laws Diploma conferred on George Washington, 3 April 1776

Ink on parchment. H. 44 x 56 cm.
Lent by the Library of Congress

On 3 April 1776, shortly after Washington had driven the British forces from Boston, the Harvard Corporation and Overseers met in Watertown and voted to award the general the degree of Doctor of Laws as an "expression of the gratitude of this College for his eminent services in the cause of his country & to this society."[1] The LL.D., always an honorary degree at Harvard, had been given only once before, to John Winthrop in 1773.

President Langdon wrote the degree in Latin, and all members of the Corporation signed it, with the exception of John Hancock who was in Philadelphia. Samuel Cooper hastened it to Washington's headquarters the next morning, but the general had already departed for New York.

Washington was honored for leaving his home in Virginia to "deliver *New-England* from the unjust and cruel Arms of Britain, and defend the other Colonies. . . ." The newspapers printed the diploma in both Latin and English. Part of the text lists General Washington's accomplishments:

> Who, by the most signal Smiles of Divine Providence on his Military Operations, drove the Fleet and Troops of the Enemy with disgraceful Precipitation from the town of Boston, which for eleven Months had been shut up, fortified, and defended by a Garrison of above seven Thousand Regulars; so that the Inhabitants, who suffered a great Variety of Hardships and Cruelties while under the Power of their Oppressors, now rejoice in their Deliverance, the neighbouring Towns are freed from the Tumults of Arms, and our University has the agreeable Prospect of being restored to its antient Seat.[2]

According to custom, Washington's name was added to the foot of the class in which he would have been, had he attended Harvard (Class of 1749). Other revolutionary war leaders to be honored by Harvard included: Maj. Gen. Horatio Gates (LL.D. 1779); Maj. Gen. Benjamin Lincoln (A.M. 1780); Maj. Gen. John Sullivan (A.M. 1780); and Maj. Gen. Lafayette (LL.D. 1784).[3]

---

1. Corporation Records, 2:432 1/2. Harvard University Archives.
2. *Sibley's,* 12:503.
3. Kimball C. Elkins, "Honorary Degrees at Harvard," p. 33.

Senatus Academiæ Cantabrigiensis in Nov- Anglia omnibus in Christo Fidelibus ad quos Literæ præsentes pervenerint, Salutem in Domino sempiternam ————

Cum eum in finem Gradus Academici instituti fuerint, ut Viri scientia, sapientia, et virtute insignes, qui de re literaria et de republica optime meruerunt, honoribus hisce laureatis remunerarentur — Maxime decet ut honore tali afficiatur Vir illustrissimus Georgius Washington, Armiger, Exercitus Coloniarum in America fæderatarum Imperator præclarus, cujus Scientia et Amor Patriæ undique patent; qui, propter eximias Virtutes tam civiles quam militares, primum, a civibus suis Legatus electus, in Consessu celeberrimo Americano de Libertate ad extremum periclitata et Salute publica fideliter et peritissime consuluit; deinde, postulante Patria, Sedem in Virginia amœnissimam et res proprias perlubenter reliquit, ut per omnes Castrorum Labores et Pericula, nulla mercede accepta, Nov- Angliam ab armis Britannorum iniquis et crudelibus liberaret, et Colonias cæteras tueretur; et qui, sub Auspiciis Divinis maxime spectandis, ab Urbe Bostonia, per undecim Menses clausa, munita et plusquam septem millium Militum præsidio formata, Naves et Copias Hostium in fugam præcipitem et probrosam deturbavit; adeo ut Cives, plurimis divitiis et sævitiis oppressi, tandem salvi latentur, Villæ vicinæ quiescant, atque Sedibus suis Academia nostra restituatur.

Sciatis igitur quod Nos Præses et Socii Collegii Harvardini in Cantabrigia Nov- Anglorum (consentientibus honorandis admodum et reverendis Academiæ nostræ Inspectoribus) Dominum supradictum, summo honore dignum, Georgium Washington, Doctorem utriusque Juris, tam Naturæ et Gentium, tum Civilis, statuimus et creavimus; eique simul dedimus et concessimus omnia Jura, Privilegia, et Honores ad istum Gradum pertinentia.

In cujus Rei Testimonium Nos, communi Sigillo Universitatis hisce Literis affixo, Chirographa apposuimus Die tertio Aprilis, Anno Salutis millesimo septingentesimo septuagesimo sexto.

Sam.ˡ Langdon S.T.D. Præses

Nathanael Appleton S.T.D.

Joh.ˢ Winthrop LL.D. Math. Phil. Prof.

Andreas Eliot S.T.D.

Sam.ᵉ Cooper S.T.D.

Joh.ˢ Wadsworth Log. et Eth. Præc.

} Socii

Thesaurarius

46. Langdon, Samuel (1722/3-1802)

Government Corrupted by Vice, and Recovered by Righteousness . . .

Watertown: Benjamin Edes, 1775. H. 18.5 cm.
Lent by the Houghton Library; gift of J. H. Ellis (*AC7.L2596.775g)

On 31 May 1775 Samuel Langdon preached the annual Election Day sermon in Watertown before the Provincial Congress, which had just taken charge of the government. *Government Corrupted by Vice . . .* was aimed at the Tory judges and mandamus councillors:

> . . . men in whom we can have no confidence, — whose principles are subversive of our liberties — whose aim is to exercise lordship over us, and share among themselves the public wealth: — men who are ready to serve any master, and execute the most unrighteous decrees for high wages, . . . are to be set over us as counsellors and judges, at the pleasure of those who have the riches and power of the nation in their hands, and whose noblest plan is to subjugate the Colonies first, and then the whole nation to their will (pp. 6-7).

Langdon blasted the British administration for its corruption, extravagance, and its other vices which, he said, were shaming the king. He prayed that God would show the ministers their errors:

> May the eyes of the King be opened to see the ruinous tendency of the measures into which he has been led, and his heart inclined to treat his American Subjects with justice and clemency, instead of forcing them still farther to the last extremities! (p. 19).

A

SERMON.

I S A I A H 1. 26.

And I will restore thy Judges as at the first, and thy Counsellors as at the beginning : afterward thou shalt be called the City of Righteousness, the faithful City.

SHALL we rejoice, my Fathers and Brethren, or shall we weep together, on the return of this Anniversary, which from the first settlement of this Colony has been sacred to Liberty, to perpetuate that invaluable privilege of chusing, from among ourselves, wise men, fearing God, and hating covetousness, to be honorable Counsellors, to constitute one essential branch of that happy government which was established on the faith of royal Charters ?

On this day, the people have from year to year assembled, from all our town in a vast congregation,

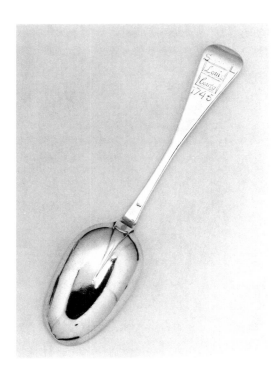

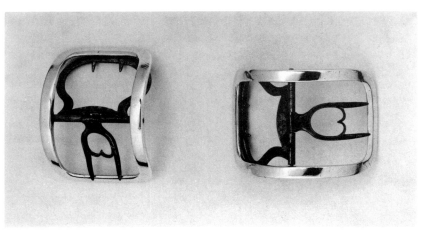

47. WHITTEMORE, William (1710-1770), American

Spoon, 1745

Silver. L. 19.3 cm.
Inscribed, back of handle: S ·:· L / Louis / bourg / 1745
Mark, back of handle: *Whittemore* in plain cartouche
Provenance: Langdon family
Harvard University; gift of Miss Anne C. Langdon (31.1959)

On 16 June 1745 Sir William Pepperrell led a force of over four thousand New England colonists who captured and looted Fort Louisbourg (on Cape Breton Island, Nova Scotia) from the French. Samuel Langdon, then twenty-two years of age, was there as chaplain of the New Hampshire regiment. (He later served as chaplain of the Continental Army, while it was in Cambridge.)

The spoon is said to have been made of silver from the spoils of the Louisbourg expedition by William Whittemore, Pepperrell's nephew. Whittemore was perhaps the most famous New Hampshire silversmith at that time, working in Portsmouth. After 1754 he moved to Kittery, Maine, where he continued to make silver boxes, spoons, and churchware.

48. DROWNE, Samuel (1749-1815), American

Pair of Shoe Buckles

Silver. H. 4.5 x 6.5 cm.
Mark, back: S ˣ Drowne (script) in plain cartouche
Provenance: Langdon family
Harvard University; gift of Miss Anne C. Langdon (32.1957a+b)

This pair of shoe buckles were once owned and worn by Samuel Langdon. They were made by Samuel Drowne, a silversmith from Portsmouth, New Hampshire. He was also a representative (1796, 1797) and selectman (1800) for that town. In 1774, he helped Capt. Thomas Pickery, his brother-in-law, obtain the gunpowder from Fort William and Mary. He served in Col. John Langdon's Company of the Light Horse in 1778.

49. COLES, John, Sr. (ca. 1749-1809), American

John Hancock (1737-1793), ca. 1795

Etching and engraving. Oval portrait pasted to decorative inscription sheet. Hand-colored with watercolor and gouache. Portrait: Oval H. 13.7 x 10 cm.; sheet H. 34.7 x 23.5 cm.

Inscribed, in arc above portrait: The MAN whom the PEOPLE delighted to Honour; on motto ribbon below portrait: FIRST PRESIDENT OF THE AMERICAN CONGRESS; below design area: His Excelly JOHN HANCOCK Esqr / late Governor and Commander in chief of the / COMMONWEALTH OF MASSACHUSETTS.

Lent by Harvard University Archives; bequest of Dr. William Richardson.

A rising political figure, John Hancock, like his uncle Thomas before him, was a liberal benefactor of Harvard College — donating books, carpet, and wallpaper for Harvard Hall's Library and Philosophy Chamber. Thus, when the members of Harvard's Corporation appointed him treasurer of the College in 1773, they thought they were being politically and financially astute. But the move turned out to be a disaster.

Once Hancock had the College's bonds, funds, and record books, Harvard became entangled in his complex financial affairs. He refused to open the books to the Corporation or to settle his accounts. In November 1774 Harvard decided to stop giving College monies to Hancock. Instead, President Langdon was authorized to receive the income from rents and donations.

At one point Harvard's treasurer was not heard from in over a year. Langdon persistently wrote Hancock trying to persuade him to settle and to turn over the books which he feared would be destroyed (cat. no. 50). Mr. Hancock was just as determined to keep the account books and funds. He resented the president's letters and wrote that

> However great the Gentlemen may think the Burden upon his Mind may bee, Mr. Hancock is not Disposed to look upon it in that light, nor shall the College suffer any Detriment in his absence.[1]

In 1776 Hancock had William Winthrop, whom he had appointed his deputy, bring the books and papers to him in Philadelphia. In 1777 the Corporation sent Tutor Stephen Hall to Philadelphia to retrieve some of the records. Later that year, Hancock's attorney delivered to Harvard some £16,000 of bonds, notes, and mortgages. But the accounts were still not settled, and no one but Hancock knew how much money he had not turned over to the College. Hancock refused to resign, considering the Corporation's censure both "severe and unmerited." He was further insulted when, on 16 July 1777, Harvard chose Ebenezer Storer, who would "constantly reside in the State," as its treasurer.

Harvard's attempts to settle its accounts continued, as the College tried to appease John Hancock, who was so angry that he transferred two young men he was supporting to Yale.[2] Although the Corporation had thought several times of suing Hancock, now governor, they decided instead to award him an LL.D. degree in 1782.

On 20 October 1783 Hancock offered to provide the Yard with a new fence to replace the one torn down by the soldiers in 1775/76. The offer was made despite the "illiberal . . . treatment" he had received "from some of the former and present Governors of the College."[3] The fence was not built, however, probably because the carpenters had demanded payment in advance.

The balance that Hancock owed Harvard was computed to be over £1000. Even though the former treasurer continued to live extravagantly, he never made his payment to the College. In 1795 his heirs paid the simple interest on the debt and promised to pay the principal within seven years. The College was finally able to recover most of its money. And, in the nineteenth century, John Langdon Sibley found most of the record books in the loft of the Hancock stables.[4]

John Coles, Sr. worked as a printer, publisher, and her-

aldry painter in Boston during the late eighteenth and early nineteenth centuries. The practice of ornamenting possessions with heraldry fell sharply during the Revolution, since many of the clients were Loyalists. But when prosperity returned to New England at the end of the eighteenth century, coats of arms were once again in demand by Boston's prominent families.

Coles sometimes printed the armorial helmets and shields in advance, and later filled in the appropriate name and motto, using Guillum's *Display of Heraldry*. If there were no direct reference to the family in Guillum, Coles adapted a coat of arms to the name and used the American flag as the crest.[5]

This memorial portrait of John Hancock, which resembles Copley's late portrait of him (cat. no. 4), was most likely executed by John Coles, Sr., and was widely circulated around New England. There is an identical memorial owned by the New England Historic Genealogical Society, Boston.

---

1. *Sibley's*, 13:429. John Hancock to Samuel Langdon, 11 April 1775. This letter is in Harvard University Archives.
2. Morison, *Three Centuries*, p. 155.
3. *Ibid*.
4. *Sibley's*, 13:445.
5. Walter Kendall Watkins, "John Coles, Heraldry Painter," p. 136; and Harold Bowditch, "Early Water-Color Paintings of New England Coats of Arms," pp. 190-94.

50. Langdon, Samuel

Autograph letter, signed, to John Hancock. Cambridge, 3 April 1775

Ink on cream antique laid paper. Folded, leaf: 31 x 19 cm.
Watermark: Coat of arms of Great Britain
Lent by Harvard University Archives; bequest of Charles P. Greenough

This is one of many futile letters that President Langdon wrote in an effort to persuade Treasurer Hancock to settle the College's accounts. While acknowledging the demands placed on Hancock by his "Patriotic exertions," Langdon reminded the treasurer of his obligations to the Board of Overseers and "to the World."

Langdon suggested that, while Hancock was attending the Continental Congress, and therefore unable to take care of College business, the treasurer's papers be turned over to the Corporation.

A more urgent message, written in a postscript dated 6 April 1775, appears on the second sheet of this letter:

> The news we have just received gives me great concern to have our College papers, etc. removed from Boston immediately ~ May not this be done without delay, even though you cannot now attend to the settlement of accompts? If you think proper to send an Order for the delivery of them, to one of your Clerks, I will give him a receipt to his satisfaction, & take proper care of everything until you can see the Corporation ~ I find it is the general apprehension, that it will be most prudent for the inhabitants of Boston to remove their valuable ~~objects~~ effects out of town as soon as ~~possible~~ they can. Certainly therefore, the College estate ought to be taken care of among the best.

51. Derived from an unknown original

Ebenezer Storer (1730-1807), Treasurer of Harvard College 1777-1807

Pastel and watercolor over photograph. Image: Oval: H. 17.7 x 13
cm.; sheet: H. 22.7 x 18 cm.
Provenance: Francis Storer Eaton
Harvard University Portrait Collection; gift of Francis Storer Eaton
(H 558)

Ebenezer Storer (A.B. 1747) was a Boston merchant, Harvard benefactor, and deacon of the Brattle Square Church. A Patriot, he signed the non-importation agreement and became involved in the publication of the Hutchinson-Oliver Letters, an episode which may have led to his resignation as deacon in 1773. When the war broke out, he left Boston to spend the winter in Needham.

During the war, the Corporation asked Storer to become treasurer of the College. The college funds were in chaos, due to the different types of currency in circulation and the problems left behind by John Hancock. Storer became treasurer in 1777, and held the office until his death in 1807. As treasurer, he was as conscientious as Hancock was remiss; and he succeeded, amidst wild currency fluctuations, in placing the College on a solid financial footing.

His second wife, Hannah Quincy (cat. no. 29), widow of Dr. Bela Lincoln, was the daughter of Col. Josiah Quincy (cat. no. 21). When Storer's various businesses suffered from the war and his labors on Harvard's behalf, the family exerted its influence for him. In 1797 Pres. John Adams appointed Storer to the post of inspector of Massachusetts District Three of the Excise Office of the United States. He also served for two years as the treasurer and collector of taxes for Boston. The positions provided him with the regular income he required to support his family.

52. American, 18th century

Desk

Mahogany banded with satinwood. Box: H. 26, W. 70.5, D. 45.5 cm.;
    Stand: H. 71, W. 71, D. 46 cm.
Provenance: Francis Storer Eaton
Harvard University; gift of Amelia Peabody, 1949

This desk belonged to Treasurer Ebenezer Storer. The box opens to form a slanted writing surface which was once covered with gold-tooled red leather (now with red baize inset). The desk is hinged at the center to give access to the compartments below. There are three shallow drawers at the rear.

The box can be carried by the brass bail handles on each side, or rested upon the five-legged stand. The extra leg at right front swings forward with the right half of the apron to support the open desk. There is a drawer with a bail handle to the right, plus a writing slide to the left side of the stand.

53. FERGUSON, James (1710-1776), English

Terrestrial Globe, ca. 1744-1771

Globe: Cardboard built up with plaster of Paris and covered with
colored paper. Case: Shagreen. Globe: DIAM. 7.1 cm.; case 7.9 cm.
Inscribed, within cartouche: A New/ GLOBE of the/ Earth/ by James
Ferguson
Provenance: Francis Storer Eaton
Lent by Harvard University Library

This portable terrestrial globe and its case (which opens
up to show the heavens) also belonged to Ebenezer Storer.
It was given to Harvard in 1914, along with other Storer
memorabilia, including his Yale and Harvard degrees, by
his great-grandson Francis Storer Eaton.

The globe, together with its case, was made by James
Ferguson, a fellow of the Royal Society. It traces the voyage of Lord George Anson (1697-1762) which began in
1740 and lasted until 1744. It does not, however, show
any of the areas that Capt. James Cook (1728-1779)
discovered on his famous voyages and thus was probably made before Cook's return in 1771 from his first
expedition.[1]

Although Ferguson studied electricity, mechanics, drawings in perspective, and portrait painting, his main interest
lay in astronomy. He devised an "astronomical Rotula,"
and an orrery, and invented an "eclipsareon," and other
scientific instruments. In 1761 he observed the transit of
Venus and, in 1764, a partial solar eclipse.

1. This information was supplied by David Wheatland and Ebenezer
Gay, Collection of Historical Scientific Instruments, Harvard
University.

54. REVERE, Paul (1735-1818), American, after Joseph
Chadwick (ca. 1721-1783), American

A Westerly View of the Colledges in Cambridge New England, 1767

Copper plate line engraving on tan (discolored) antique laid paper.
H. 26.5 x 41.5 cm.
Watermark: J Whatman
Inscribed, in lower margin: l.l.: Josh Chadwick, del — ; l.r.: P Revere
Sculp.; l.c.: A Westerly View of the Colledges in Cambridge New
England / A Harvard Hall   B Stoughton   C Massachusetts   D
Hollis   E   Holden Chapel
Provenance: Matthew A. Stickney
Lent by Harvard University Archives; gift of Francis R. Appleton,
James B. Ayer, Ezra H. Baker, Henry W. Cunningham, William
Endicott, Frederick L. Gay, and Grenville H. Norcross (HUV 2167)

This engraving shows Harvard as it looked in the late
1760s. The College consisted of the new Harvard Hall
(cat. no. 56), Stoughton Hall, Massachusetts Hall (cat. no.
57), Hollis Hall (cat. no. 91), and Holden Chapel. A low
fence surrounded the Yard but allowed two entrances, one
for pedestrians and one for carriages. The governor's
four-horse coach is seen in the foreground of the engraving, symbolizing the relationship between College and
Province.[1] Gentlemen and ladies are seen conversing or
riding horseback, while scholars walk through the Yard
in their long academic robes.

The building to the far left was Harvard's first independent chapel. Ironically, though the college trained the colony's ministers, until 1741 it did not have its own chapel
where morning and evening prayers could be heard.[2] But
in that year Thomas Hutchinson, in London on colonial
business, received a gift for the College of £400 to build a
chapel. The donation came from the widow of Samuel
Holden, an English Dissenter, merchant, member of Parliament, and director of the Bank of England.[3]

Work began on the brick chapel in 1742, and was completed two years later. The building, which may have been

designed in England, was elegant, yet plain, save for the
wooden pediments carved with the Holden coat of arms.
For twenty-two years it served as the college chapel, and
in it students witnessed public admonitions — and sometimes whippings — during the services.[4]

In 1766 a chapel was set aside in the new Harvard Hall,
and Holden was abandoned as a place of worship. The
Massachusetts House of Representatives met in the building for three years (1769-1772). During the war, it served
as barracks for 160 soldiers, who seriously damaged it. It
was next used as a carpentry shop and storage room for
the college fire equipment. It became the first location for
Harvard's Medical School in 1783, and in the nineteenth
century was renovated to accommodate a chemistry laboratory and anatomical museum. It has since been restored to its original condition and used as a club house,
a choir rehearsal hall, and general auditorium.[5]

To the right of Holden Chapel, between Harvard and Massachusetts, is Stoughton Hall, the gift of Gov. William Stoughton (A.B. 1650).[6] On 3 March 1698 the Harvard Corporation appointed a committee "to treat wth the Honourable Lieu^t Govern^r about ye additional building to ye Colledg, of wch his Hono^r has made some Proposals to ye Corporation."[7] Completed in 1699/1700 by master builder Thomas Willis, at a cost of £1,000, Stoughton Hall contained sixteen chambers, one especially reserved for the nearest relative of the governor.

The building soon began to decay and needed substantial repairs as early as 1710. In 1721 a mason pronounced it unsafe and advised that it be torn down. Nonetheless, it served as a dormitory until the Revolution, when 240 soldiers were quartered there. In addition, one room was given to Samuel and Ebenezer Hall as quarters for their patriotic newspaper, the *New England Chronicle*. The College began dismantling Stoughton Hall in 1779 and tried unsuccessfully to sell it at auction in October 1781. Finally, on 13 November 1781, the Corporation voted that "Deacon Aaron Hill have the liberty to take down the walls of Stoughton Hall. . . ."[8] A new Stoughton was erected in 1804/05.

This view, dated 1767, was drawn by Joseph Chadwick, an artillery officer, surveyor, and engineer. It is likely that he drew plans for Boston's fortifications, and it is known that he was in that city in 1767.

The engraver of this rare print (less than a half dozen have been located) was Paul Revere. Revere's Day Book, which contained his charge accounts, recorded on 4 July 1767: "Capt. Josep Chadwick Dr / To one half of the Engravings a Plate / for a Perspective View of the Colleges / To Printing / 4-0-0."[9]

Revere was one of Boston's finest craftsmen. He not only produced sumptuous pieces of silver, but engraved portraits, political cartoons, bookplates, and advertising cards on copper. During the war he manufactured gunpowder, cast cannon, participated in the Penobscot expedition and engraved and printed currency and treasurer's notes. In May 1775 Revere was commissioned by the Provincial Congress to engrave paper bills totaling £26,000 for the soldiers' advance pay. For the twenty-, fourteen-, and six-shilling notes, Revere used the reverse side of a portion of the copper plate on which he had engraved the view of Harvard College.

After the Revolution, Revere continued as a silversmith, and also opened a hardware store and established an iron foundry. The Revere Copper Company furnished not only the brass and copper for the ship *Constitution*, but also the copper for the State House dome.

1. William C. Lane, "Early Views of Harvard College," p. 351.
2. The students always observed the Sabbath at the Congregational meetinghouse (cat. no. 81) nearby.
3. From 1730 until his death in 1740, Holden had given £500 through Rev. Benjamin Colman to various institutions, including Harvard.
4. H. A. Clas and F. O. Vaille, *The Harvard Book,* 1:59.
5. Samuel Batchelder, *Bits of Harvard History,* pp. 3-30.
6. Stoughton is perhaps best remembered as a judge in the Salem witch trials.
7. Bail, *Views of Harvard,* p. 26.
8. *Ibid.,* p. 30.
9. Clarence S. Brigham, *Paul Revere's Engravings,* p. 40.

55. ABBOT, John (1777-1854), American
College Buildings, 1798

Gouache and pencil on cream laid paper. Image: Oval: H. 41 x 28
   cm.; sheet: 58 x 42.4 cm., irregular
Inscribed, u.c.: Harvard; l.l.: Holden, Hollis; l.r.: Massachusetts Hall
Lent by Harvard University Archives; gift of John William Pitt Abbot
   (HUV 2197)

The College buildings represented in this oval view are
Holden Chapel, Hollis Hall, Harvard Hall, and Massachusetts Hall. In between Massachusetts and Harvard,
one can see in the distance the yellow parsonage. First
erected by the town of Cambridge in 1670 "for the entertainment of the minister that the Lord may please to send
us," the parsonage had been rebuilt and enlarged in 1720.
For sixty-seven years it was the home of Rev. Nathaniel
Appleton (cat. no. 82).

In addition to the overall view of the College, John Abbot
(A.B. 1798) executed individual watercolors depicting
Hollis, Harvard, and Massachusetts Halls. Abbot, a native of Westford, Massachusetts, later became a lawyer
and served as state senator from Middlesex County.

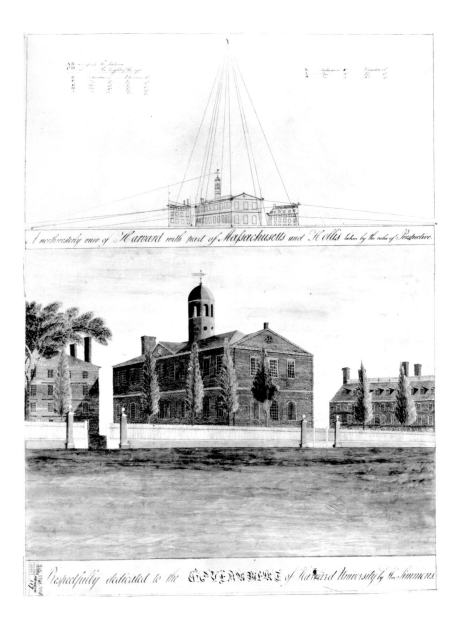

56. SIMMONS, William (1782-1843), American

Harvard, Massachusetts, and Hollis Halls, 1804

Ink and watercolor on cream wove paper. Image: H. 44 x 47 cm.;
sheet: H. 68.5 x 48.5 cm.

Inscribed, in upper margin: A northwesterly view of Harvard with
part of Massachusetts and Hollis taken by the rules of Perspective.;
in lower margin: Respectfully dedicated to the GOVERNMENT of
Harvard University by Wm. Simmons.

Lent by Harvard University Archives (HUC 8804.581pf)

This perspective view, with mathematical calculations
above, focuses on Harvard Hall, although it includes part
of Massachusetts and Hollis Halls as well.

The second Harvard Hall, built between 1672 and
1676, burned on 24 January 1764. The General Court had
been meeting there due to a smallpox epidemic in Boston,
and sparks from a fire left burning overnight set the building aflame.[1] The finest library in America, as well as Harvard's scientific apparatus, portraits of its benefactors,
and the museum, with its "curiosities, natural and arti-
ficial," were lost.

President Holyoke sent a message on 1 February 1764
to the students, who were on winter vacation, not to return to the College until notified. He advised them in the
meantime to "diligently follow their Studies under the Influence and Direction of the Minister or Ministers of the
several Towns to which they belong, or any other Gentlemen of Learning that they may converse with."[2]

Appeals for assistance went out to friends in New England and Britain. The General Court somewhat belatedly
presented the College with £100 for a "Water Engine,"
and reimbursed the students for their losses. The Province
appropriated £2000 for construction of a new Harvard
Hall (final cost was over £6000), which was built by
Thomas Dawes according to Gov. Francis Bernard's design. The new building, erected on the site of Old Harvard
Hall, was completed in 1766.

Unlike its predecessor, the new building had only public rooms. The basement contained the kitchen and buttery. A large hall on the first floor was divided into a chapel and a dining hall. On the second floor was the new library, the Philosophy Chamber, and two small lecture rooms called the "Mathematical School" and the "Hebrew School."

The General Court returned to Cambridge from 1769 to 1772 by order of the governor, and the Council met in the Philosophy Chamber. During the siege of Boston, American troops occupied Harvard Hall, melting into bullets some thousand pounds of lead from the roof.

Harvard Hall has been altered twice to provide space for more classrooms. In the nineteenth century, both a projection in the middle and a one-story extension across the front were added. About 1965 the interior of Harvard Hall was drastically remodelled.

William Simmons (A.B. 1804), a native of Hanover, New Hampshire, submitted this mathematical thesis for the Exhibition of 1804. He later practiced law in Boston and was said to be "respected for his high moral worth and unimpeachable integrity."[3]

1. Although Massachusetts, Hollis, and Stoughton Halls and Holden Chapel also caught fire, all were saved but Harvard Hall.
2. F. Apthorp Foster, "The Burning of Harvard Hall, 1764, and Its Consequences," *Publications of the Colonial Society of Massachusetts* 14(1911):5.
3. Bail, *Views of Harvard,* p. 108.

57. Artist Unknown

Massachusetts Hall, ca. 1806-07

Watercolor and pen on cream laid paper. Image: H. 37.4 x 28 cm.; sheet: H. 35.3 x 47 cm.
Inscribed, below margin, l.c.: A North West View of Massachusetts Hall; l.r.: No. 1
Lent by Harvard University Archives (HUV 2206)

In 1717, the College found need to expand, since "the Numbers of yᵉ Sons of yᵉ Prophets are now so increas'd, that the Place where they were wont to dwell is become so Streight as not to be capable of receiving yᵐ."[1] Harvard petitioned the General Court that year for assistance in erecting a new "college" and, in May 1718, the legislature agreed to finance a building three stories high, fifty feet long, and fifty feet wide, which has become known as Massachusetts Hall. Committees were appointed to choose the site (Massachusetts Hall, together with Harvard and Stoughton Halls, formed a quadrangle which opened toward the Common) and to oversee construction. After much debate over size, the Court finally — in mid-construction — approved a new plan extending the length an additional fifty feet.

On 18 November 1720, the building having been completed, the College thanked the Province for the "fine and goodly House" which "will be a lasting Monument, if God please, of the Just Regards of the Present Government for the Support of Religion and Learning amongst us in time to come."[2]

The rent from the thirty-two rooms in Massachusetts Hall (which could accommodate over sixty students and one or two tutors) was to provide much of the College's income in the eighteenth century. The simple brick building served as a student dormitory for over 150 years, save for the year it was occupied by American soldiers. Under President Kirkland, the lower floor was divided up among recitation rooms and rooms for College societies. A shortage of classrooms in 1870 necessitated further renovation

A North West View of MASSACHUSETTS HALL.

58. MARTIN, Benjamin (1714-1752), English

Surveyor's Level, 1765

Brass level with telescope and compass, mounted on mahogany
tripod. H. (including tripod) 167 cm.; telescope: L. 62.2 cm.; level:
L. 25.4 cm.
Inscribed, on compass rose: B. Martin London.
Lent by the Collection of Historical Scientific Instruments (No. 68)

This surveyor's level, listed as a "Siphon Spirit Level Compleat with: Mahogony Leggs & Parallel Plates," arrived
in 1765 with a shipment of apparatus from London.

It was most likely used by the students of Rev. Samuel
Williams (third Hollis Professor of Mathematics and Natural Philosophy), who studied surveying and initiated the
practice of submitting surveys of Cambridge Common or
perspective views of Cambridge and Harvard buildings as
mathematical theses. Some of the students' projects are
displayed in this exhibition, and are invaluable in giving
us a picture of Harvard and Cambridge in the late eighteenth and early nineteenth centuries.

The level may have also been put into service during
the revolutionary war, when Harvard lent instruments to
a Massachusetts militia company to survey a line between
the American and British positions.

Benjamin Martin was a British mathematician and teacher
who invented and made scientific instruments, several of
which still exist at Harvard.

to provide two large halls for lecture rooms, laboratories,
and examination rooms. Massachusetts Hall became a
dormitory again after a fire in 1924, and in 1939, it was
remodeled to serve as offices for the president.

Massachusetts Hall was nearly a century old when this
view was drawn by an anonymous artist, ca. 1806/07. It
is the oldest surviving building at Harvard; in fact, it is the
oldest college building in America, except for the "Great
Building of the College" at William and Mary.[3]

---

1. William C. Lane, "The Building of Massachusetts Hall, 1717-
   1720," pp. 89-90.
2. *Ibid.*, pp. 109-11.
3. Bail, *Views of Harvard,* p. 30.

59. NAIRNE, Edward (1726-1806), English

Protractor, ca. 1764

Brass semicircle, originally silvered, with beveled edges. DIAM.: 30.5
  cm.
Inscribed, l.c.: E. Nairne LONDON.
Lent by the Collection of Historical Scientific Instruments (No. 64)

Protractors were another type of instrument used by the students for their mathematical theses. This one was constructed by Edward Nairne shortly after the 1764 fire. The engraved scale is numbered twice: 0°-180° (left to right) and 180°-0° (right to left).

Nairne was a famous British instrument maker and scientist, who worked with Joseph Priestley in building an "electrical machine" in 1782. A fellow of the Royal Society, he made several scientific instruments for Harvard, including a telescope, three compasses, a dip needle, and a chest microscope (cat. no. 100). His trade card, printed in both English and French, indicated his widespread reputation.

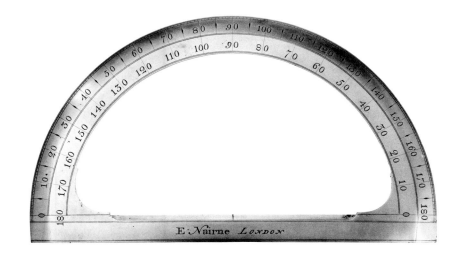

60. GREENE, Charles Winston (1783-1857), American

College House, 1801

Ink and watercolor on cream wove paper. H. 49.8x 70.3 cm., irregular
Inscribed, at top of leaf: A North-eastwardly view of the College
House taken at a small distance by the eye; in wreath, l.r.: Respect-
fully inscribed/ To the government/ Of Harvard College/ By
their obedient servant/ Charles W. Greene/ Sept. 29. 1801.
Lent by Harvard University Archives (HUC 8802.535pf)

Built around 1770 as a private home, this three-story
wooden structure (with brick ends) was located about

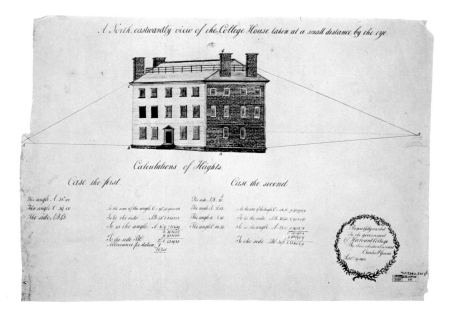

fifty feet north of the Webber House (later called College
House No. 2; see cat. no. 73), near the present Church
Street. It soon became notorious as "Wiswall's Den."

Mr. Wiswall, his ill wife, her nurse, and several children
moved into the house soon after its completion. Mrs. Wiswall died (some said because her husband dragged her up
and down the stairs by her hair), and her husband quickly
married the nurse, creating a scandal in Cambridge. While
the rest of the family was at church one Sunday, the legend
continued, the second Mrs. Wiswall began to go through
the possessions of her predecessor, which had been left to
her children. She was visited by the Devil, who shook her
"in pieces" for her crimes; she went into convulsions and
died shortly thereafter.

In 1774 the building was acquired by the College and
was used as a dormitory (until 1845/46) for those students
who could not get a room in the Yard. It served first as a
residence for freshmen who, on every anniversary of the
macabre event mentioned above, reportedly could hear
"plaintive screams" and see "flitting garments daggled
with blood."[1]

In the early nineteenth century, one could visit the
building's lower story and rent a commencement gown
from the ladies who ran a haberdasher's shop, or take advantage of the services of Marcus Remy's barber shop.
The College House was finally torn down around 1846.

This mathematical thesis, with its several calculations of
heights, was submitted for the Exhibition of 29 September
1801 by Charles Winston Greene. A native of Connecticut,
Greene (A.B. 1802) turned to business after graduation.
But financial difficulties prompted him to open a private
boarding school in Jamaica Plain. Greene later moved the
school to East Greenwich, Rhode Island, where he died
in 1857.

1. Bail, *Views of Harvard,* pp. 104-05. See also B. H. Hall, *A Collection of College Words and Customs,* p. 155.

IV. Cambridge in the Revolutionary Era

Like many other New England towns, Cambridge began its drift toward revolution with a protest in 1765 against the Stamp Act and a celebration marked by fireworks and merriment a year later when the measure was repealed. In 1772 the town declared, in a meeting concerning judges' salaries, that although

we are and ever have been ready to risk our lives and fortunes in defence of his majesty King George the Third, . . . we are as much concerned to maintain and secure our own invaluable rights and liberties . . . . But alas, with what ingratitude are we treated, how cruelly oppressed! . . . We have repeatedly petitioned our most gracious sovereign for a redress of grievances, but no redress has yet been obtained, whereby we have been almost driven to despair. . . ."[1]

By the following year, Cantabrigians were protesting the tea tax and feeling they could no longer remain "idle spectators." They were prepared, they said, to join Boston and other towns, on the shortest notice, "in any measures that may be thought proper, to deliver ourselves and posterity from Slavery."[2]

The revolutionary struggle began in Cambridge in the fall of 1774. Although most of the townspeople (approximately sixteen thousand population in total) were Patriots, there were a few Loyalists. Many of these were affluent merchants and office-holders, living in the present Brattle Street area (then nicknamed "Tory Row"). Judges Joseph Lee (A.B. 1729) and Samuel Danforth (A.B. 1715), royal appointees to the Mandamus Council, lived in Cambridge.[3] So did Lt. Gov. Thomas Oliver (see cat. no. 72), the Council's presiding officer.[4] These three men became the target of thousands of angry citizens on 1 and 2 September 1774. Only a plea for non-intervention from Thomas Oliver prevented General Gage from sending his British troops to quell the mob. The townspeople demanded and received the resignations of the three councillors. Oliver promised "as a man of honor and a Christian, that I never will hereafter upon any terms whatsoever accept a seat at said Board on the present novel and oppressive plan of government. My house [Elmwood] at Cambridge being surrounded by about four thousand people, in compliance with their command I sign my name."[5]

Shortly thereafter, the mandamus councillors fled Cambridge with other Loyalists, including Maj. John Vassall (A.B. 1757; see cat. no. 69), Attorney General Jonathan Sewall (A.B. 1748), and Col. Henry Vassall's widow (cat. no. 66). Their luxurious homes were commandeered by the Committee of Safety and leased to various individuals or used as hospitals and quarters for troops. The John Vassall house became Washington's headquarters.

The months that followed were difficult indeed. Huts and tents sprang up on the Common and supplies grew scarce as the town took on the appearance of an armed camp. Soldiers were quartered in Christ Church, in private homes, in the College buildings, or on the Common. With Harvard exiled to Concord, the Yard fence was torn down for firewood. Breastworks appeared along Quincy Street and Butler's Hill (now Dana Hill).[6] The town was thus transformed until Washington and his troops left in the early spring of 1776.

In November 1777 a new group of soldiers arrived in Cambridge. These were the "Convention Troops"—over five thousand British and Hessian soldiers, commanded by Lt. Gen. John Burgoyne, who had surrendered at Saratoga. The prisoners of war had been promised passage back to England as a condition of surrender, and they were to wait in Cambridge for transport. Their stay was not a happy one. The rank and file lived in crowded, drafty barracks on Winter and Prospect Hills in Somerville, then part of Charlestown, since Cambridge residents would not allow the troops into their homes. Nor would Harvard College turn over its buildings, although they were empty for most of the winter during the students' long vacation.[7] The soldiers were charged exorbitant prices for food and other necessities by the shopkeepers.

Life was not quite so dismal for "Gentleman Johnny" Burgoyne and his top officers. They could afford to rent the elegant mansions vacated earlier by the Tories. They hunted, raced horses, gambled, and partied. Apthorp House was occupied by Burgoyne. The Sewall-Lechmere House became the social center for the German contingent, with General and Mrs. von Riedesel giving dances and dinners for their officers.

In April 1778 Burgoyne went to Newport and from there back to England. But Congress refused to repatriate the troops. They remained in Cambridge until 11 November 1778 when they were sent on a march that took them to Charlottesville, Virginia, where they spent the remainder of the war years.

In most ways Cambridge was little affected by the Revolution after 1776. The battles took place elsewhere, and life went on much as before, except that an entire layer of society had been removed. Some Loyalists, like Judge Lee and General Brattle, were able to retain or bequeath their estates, but most saw them confiscated by the new government. The Vassalls and their connections, resident in Cambridge but supported by plantations in the West Indies, left America forever, leaving the Georgian mansions on Brattle Street as their monument.

1. Lucius R. Paige, *History of Cambridge, Massachusetts, 1630-1877*, 1:144. This was sent to Capt. Thomas Gardner, Cambridge's representative in the General Assembly, on 14 December 1772.

2. *Ibid.*, p. 149. This resolution was passed at a meeting held on 26 November 1773.

3. On 17 June 1774, General Gage dissolved the General Court. The governor and his Tory mandamus councillors ruled as much of the Province as his troops controlled. In October of that year, the members of the House of Representatives resolved themselves into the Provincial Congress.

4. Thomas Oliver was no relation to former Lt. Gov. Andrew or Chief Justice Peter Oliver.

5. Paige, *History of Cambridge*, 1:156.

6. *Ibid.*, 2:241 and Samuel Batchelder, *Bits of Harvard History*, pp. 250-55.

7. Samuel Batchelder, "Burgoyne and His Officers in Cambridge, 1777-1778," pp. 52-53.

61. LILLIE, Rupert Ballou (1907-   ), American

A Pictorial Map of Cambridge 1760-1770, 1939

Water-colored pen drawing mounted on panel. H. 66 x 96.5 cm.
Inscribed, in cartouche, l.c.: A / PICTORIAL MAP / OF / CAMBRIDGE / 1760-1770 / SHOWING THE RESIDENCES & GARDENS / OF THE PRIN-CIPAL CITIZENS OF THE TOWN / (scale) / NAMES SHOWN IN PAREN-THESIS INDICATE THOSE PERSONS DWELLING HERE AT ANOTHER PERIOD. / DATES INDICATE EXISTING BUILDINGS & / THE TIME OF THEIR ERECTION, / BY / RUPERT B. LILLIE
Lent by Harvard University Archives (HUV 2160)

This map, based on the Pelham Map, was drawn by Rupert B. Lillie (M.L.A. 1935).[1] It depicts the town of Cambridge around 1760-70 and shows not only the more famous buildings — Harvard College, Christ Church, and the Tory Row mansions — but also includes houses of professors and yeomen, the blacksmith shop, jail, burying ground, tanyard, orchards, pastures, and taverns.

The main approach from Boston to Cambridge was "ye Great Bridge," spanning the Charles River at the site of the present Larz Anderson Bridge. Schooners were able to sail up the river and dock near the bridge to deliver supplies to the town and College. A causeway crossing over the marsh and creek led into town.[2]

---

1. The Pelham Map, drawn by Henry Pelham (1749-1806; half-brother of John Singleton Copley), and published in London in 1777, depicts Boston Harbor, and includes Cambridge and parts of other nearby towns. Mr. Lillie was responsible for the historical research connected with the construction of the dioramas in Widener Library.
2. Rupert B. Lillie, *Cambridge in 1775*, p. 8.

62. COPLEY, John Singleton (1738-1815), American

William Brattle (1706-1776), 1756

Oil on canvas. H. 126 x 100 cm. Signed and dated, l.l.: John:S:Copley. Pinx/1756
Anonymous Loan

William Brattle (A.B. 1722) was placed at the head of his class at Harvard due to his family's prominence.[1] His father William was the pastor of the Cambridge Church; his uncle Thomas was treasurer of the College; and he inherited their large estates while still a young man.

After graduation, Brattle tried preaching, medicine, and law. It is said, however, that he did not excel in any of them, being far too busy with his many civil offices. He served as justice of the peace, representative, member of the Council, and for twenty-one terms as a Cambridge selectman. Likewise, he climbed through the ranks of the militia, climaxing his military career in 1773 with an appointment as major general. A member of the Harvard Board of Overseers, he served on committees to build Hollis Hall in 1762 and rebuild Harvard Hall in 1764.

Initially, "Brigadier Brattle" sided with the Whig party, partly, it is said, because of his disappointment at not having been named chief justice, a post which went instead to Thomas Hutchinson. He was friendly with the Sons of Liberty and worked with them in the House of Representatives. But, sometime in 1773 or 1774, he switched to the side of the Loyalists.

Brattle's troubles began soon thereafter. General Gage ordered him to investigate the complaints concerning the removal of ammunition from the Medford powder house by the townspeople. On 29 August 1774 Brattle made his report in a letter to Gage which the general dropped on the streets of Boston. It came into the hands of the Whig leadership who promptly published it as a broadside (cat. no. 63A).

The Patriots blamed Brattle for Gage's order to remove

the remaining guns and powder to Castle William. Mobs plundered the Brattle home in Cambridge and Brattle fled to Boston, narrowly escaping gunfire aimed at him near the Brighton bridge.

On 2 September Brattle issued an explanation for his behavior and asked forgiveness (see cat. no. 63B). He could not return to Cambridge, however, and remained in Boston until 1776, when he left for Halifax with the British troops. He died in Halifax that year.

The following description of him, as he presided over the Ancient & Honorable Artillery Company election in 1774, sounds almost as if it were based on the Copley portrait which, however, was painted twenty years earlier:

> Dressed in a superb suit of scarlet, trimmed with broad gold lace, with a campaign wig, gold laced hat, and a very handsome sword, he presented a most gorgeous spectacle. He performed his part with great propriety, though accompanied with some degree of pomposity.[2]

Jules Prown has pointed out that this is one of the first Copley male portraits to be influenced by Blackburn, as seen in the high rosy flesh color of the face, the yellowish cast of highlights, and the light palette.[3]

---

1. A Harvard student's class rank in the early and mid-eighteenth century was not determined by scholastic achievement, but by social or official rank of his parents. When the fall term began, the college steward placed the freshmen in temporary seniority. Their places were permanently assigned by the faculty the following March or April. Students who entered late or transferred were put at the foot of the class. Being degraded several notches — or to the bottom — was often a punishment for misconduct, although a student was usually restored to his original position after a public confession. Alphabetical listing of students began after 1769.

2. *Sibley's,* 7:20.

3. Jules David Prown, *John Singleton Copley,* 1:23.

63A. **Broadside.** Letter from General Brattle to General Gage, 29 August 1774

Printed on laid paper. H. 19 x 24 cm.

B. **Broadside.** Letter from General Brattle to General Gage and General Brattle's Address to the Public, 2 September 1774

Printed on laid paper. H. 35.5 x 21 cm.
Lent by the Massachusetts Historical Society, Boston

Dated 29 August 1774, this copy of Brattle's letter to General Gage was circulated throughout Massachusetts:

> . . . Capt. Minot of Concord . . . informed Mr Brattle that there had been repeatedly made pressing Applications to him to warn his Company to meet at one Minute's Warning Equipt with Arms and Ammunition according to Law, he had constantly denied them, adding, if he did not gratify them he should be constrained to quit his Farms and Town. Mr. Brattle told him he had better do that than lose his life and be handed for a Rebel . . . So there is now therein, the King's Powder only, which shall remain there, as a sacred Depositum, till ordered out by the Capt. General.

In his reply to the public, published 2 September 1774, Brattle denied having advised Gage to remove the powder. He pleaded for his neighbors' forgiveness:

> Upon the whole, the threatenings I have met with, my Banishment from my own Home, the Place of my Nativity, my House being searched, . . . yet this Grief is much lessened by the Pleasure arising in my Mind from a Consciousness that I am a Friend to my Country; and . . . that I really acted according to my best Judgment for its true Interest. I am extremely sorry for what has taken Place; I hope I may be forgiven, and desire it of all that are offended, since I acted from an honest, friendly Principle, though it might be a mistaken one.

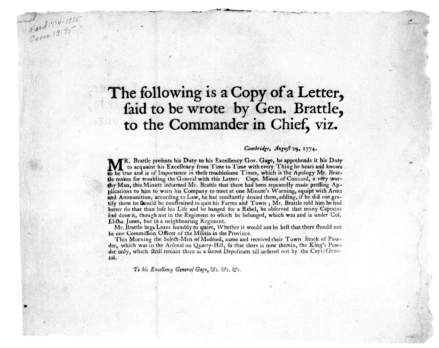

63A.

The following is a Copy of a Letter, said to be wrote by Gen. Brattle, to the Commander in Chief, viz.

Cambridge, August 29, 1774.

MR Brattle presents his Duty to his Excellency Gov. Gage, he apprehends it his Duty to acquaint his Excellency from Time to Time with every Thing he hears and knows to be true and is of Importance in these troublesome Times, which is the Apology Mr. Brattle makes for troubling the General with this Letter. Capt. Minot of Concord, a very worthy Man, this Minute informed Mr. Brattle that there had been repeatedly made pressing Applications to him to warn his Company to meet at one Minute's Warning, equipt with Arms and Ammunitions, according to Law he had constantly denied them, adding, if he did not gratify them he should be constrained to quit his Farms and Town ; Mr. Brattle told him he had better do that than lose his Life and be hanged for a Rebel, he observed that many Captains had done it, though not in the Regiment to which he belonged, which was and is under Col. Elisha Jones but in a neighbouring Regiment.

Mr. Brattle begs Leave humbly to quere, Whether it would not be best that there should not be one Commission Officer of the Militia in the Province.

This Morning the Select-Men of Medford, came and received their Town Stock of Powder, which was in the Arsenal on Quarry-Hill, so that there is now therein, the King's Powder only, which shall remain there as a sacred Depositum till ordered out by the Capt. General.

To his Excellency General Gage, &c, &c, &.

Gen. Brattle's ADDRESS To the PUBLIC.

BOSTON, September 2, 1774,

I THINK it but Justice to myself to give an Account of my Conduct, for which I am blamed ; and to obviate some Mistakes which are believed. His Excellency Governor Gage wrote me in the words following : " *Sir, as I am informed there are several Military Stores in your Charge, at Cambridge ; I beg the favour of you to send me a Return of them, as soon as convenient, specifying the different Sorts of each,* T. Gage. *To Major General Brattle.*"---Which Order I obeyed ; the like I did to Governors Pownal, Bernard and Hutchinson : In doing of which, every Soldier will say, I did but my Duty, But it is affirmed, I advised the Governor to remove the Powder? this I positively deny, because it is absolutely false.---It never so much as entered into my Mind or Thought. After I had made my Return, I never heard one Word about the Affair till the Night before last, when Sheriff Phipps came to my House, with the Governor's Order to deliver him the Powder and Guns ; the Keys of the Powder-House I then delivered him, and wrote to Mr. Mason, who had the Care of the Guns under me to deliver them, which I suppose he did ; both I imagine were taken, but were transported I know not. I wrote to the Governor what is contained in the Hand-Bill lately printed ? I did not write the Governor the Grounds and reasons of the Quere therein contained ; but I will now mention them : They proceeded from a real Regard both to the Commission Officers and to the Province : First, to the Commission Officers ; I thought and still think it was best for them ; many of whom I thought would be unwilling to issue their Warrants, and if they did not, I apprehended they might meet with some Difficulty ; and those that did, I was not convinced so great Good would result therefrom as if another Method was taken : Secondly, I thought, and still think, it would be much better for the Province ; for supposing there was not one Commission Officer for the present in it, what Damage could the Province sustain ? It may be answered, Commission Officers are supposed to be the most understanding in Military Affairs ; I grant it : But supposing their Commissions were vacated, supposing the respective Companies in the Province were disposed and determined to do any one Matter or Thing, which they imagined to be for its Safety ; and proper Persons were to be employed to lead them, &c. doth their not having Commissions in the least unfit them from being employed in the particular Services they may be chosen to execute ; and in this Way cannot any One conceive that some bad Consequenes might be possibly prevented. Is it not easy to conceive, that the Commission Officers, leading their respective Companies, might in the Eyes of the Judicious be looked upon more blameable in doing such and such Things, than they would be if they were not Military Officers, and did not act under Commission ? Might not the Difference with respect to the Province be looked upon very great both at home and here. It was suggested that General Gage demanded the Towns Stocks of Powder ; this certainly he did not, the above Order speaks for itself. As I would not have delivered the Provincial Powder to any one but to his Excellency or Order, so the Towns Stocks I would have delivered to none but to the Selectmen or their Order. Upon the whole, the Threatnings I have met with, my Banishment from my own Home, the Place of my Nativity, my House being searched, though I am informed it was without Damage, and the sense of the People, touching my Conduct, &c. for the present cannot but b egrievous, yet this Grief is much lessened by the Pleasure arising in my Mind, from a Consciousness that I am a Friend to my Country ; and, in the above Instances, that I really acted according to my best Judgment for its true Interest. I am extremely sorry for what has taken Place ; I hope I may be forgiven, and desire it of all that are offended, since I acted from an honest, friendly Principle, though it might be a Mistaken one.

W. BRATTLE.

64. Brattle House, November 1975

Photograph. H. 28 x 35 cm.
Paul Birnbaum, photographer

William Brattle built this two-story Georgian house in 1727, shortly after his marriage to Katherine Saltonstall (daughter of former governor of Connecticut Gurdon Saltonstall). The mob plundered their fashionable home in 1774, and the Provincial Congress took the remaining stores. During the Revolution, Washington's aide-de-camp and commissary-general Maj. Thomas Mifflin and his family lived in the house. For a time, they shared their quarters with fellow Philadelphians, Dr. and Mrs. John Morgan, Morgan having been named surgeon-general after Dr. Benjamin Church's arrest (see cat. no. 68).

Brattle's estate was declared insolvent at his death. Although some of the Boston lands and other properties were confiscated and sold, his children managed to hang onto the house and lands in Cambridge. His son Thomas Brattle (A.B. 1760) had spent the war years in England and Rhode Island, but he returned to the house at 42 Brattle Street following the peace.[1] He enlarged the property, which included a pond with an island and grounds extending to the river, and built one of the first greenhouses in America. The gambrel-roofed house was altered in 1891 and again in 1951, after a fire. Today it is the home of the Cambridge Center for Adult Education.

---

1. Brattle Street in the eighteenth century was variously called the Highway to Watertown, the King's Highway, Church Row, and Tory Row.

65. BLACKBURN, Joseph (fl. 1752-1763), English

Col. Henry Vassall (1721-1769), 1757

Oil on canvas. H. 76.5 x 63.8 cm. Signed and dated, l.l.: I. Blackburn
   Pinxit 1757
Inscribed, left of wig bow: Mr. Vassall
Provenance: Henry Vassall; Elizabeth Vassall Russell, his daughter;
   Rebecca Russell Pearce, her daughter; Charles Russell Pearce,
   Baltimore, her son; Elizabeth Vassall Pearce Prentiss, his daughter;
   Elizabeth Vassall Prentiss McCowen, her daughter; Richard Henry
   Dana III
Lent by the Cambridge Historical Society

Henry Vassall, the fourteenth of eighteen children, was the only boy in his family not sent to Harvard. He spent the first twenty years of his life on his family's estate in Jamaica, and although he lived in Cambridge after 1741, he continued to visit the West Indies frequently to manage his property and that of his wife, Penelope Royall Vassall (cat. no. 66), whom he married in 1742.

Although mainly a gentleman of leisure, Vassall assumed some civic responsibilities. He served in the General Court, was appointed lieutenant colonel in the Middlesex Militia, and was a founding member of Christ Church, Cambridge (see cat. no. 79), where his family tomb was built.

Although Henry Vassall had a comfortable, steady income from the family's plantations, his life style was extravagant, and he often faced financial difficulties. He was forced to mortgage and sell some of his property and borrow from his relatives. By the time of his death, in 1769, he had squandered much of his inheritance, and his estate was declared insolvent.

Family tradition attributed this painting to Copley, but stylistic evidence indicates Blackburn's hand. Recent conservation of the portrait has revealed the signature and date, which confirmed the attribution to Joseph Blackburn.

66. BLACKBURN, Joseph (fl. 1752-1763), English

Penelope Royall Vassall (Mrs. Henry Vassall, 1724-1800), ca. 1750s

Oil on canvas. H. 44.5 x 38 cm.
Provenance: Henry Vassall; Elizabeth Vassall Russell, his daughter;
Rebecca Russell Pearce, her daughter; Charles Russell Pearce,
Baltimore, her son; Elizabeth Vassall Pearce Prentiss, his daughter;
Elizabeth Vassall Prentiss McCowen, her daughter; Richard Henry
Dana III
Lent by the Cambridge Historical Society

Like her husband, Penelope Vassall was raised in luxury in the West Indies, on the Antiguan plantation of her father, Isaac Royall. Upon Royall's death in 1739, she became half-owner of the estate and an extremely wealthy woman. Her husband, Henry Vassall, managed her property, the income of which was used to support their lavish style of life.

After Henry's death, Penelope continued to live in the Cambridge house for seven more years. During the last year she saw many of her Tory friends, relatives, and neighbors driven from their homes on Brattle Street, including her nephews, Lt. Gov. Thomas Oliver and Maj. John Vassall. She fled to Boston during the winter of 1774/75, seeking the protection of the British troops there. Via Nantucket she eventually reached Antigua, but found an unhappy refuge on the now run-down plantation.

She attempted to return to Cambridge in 1781, but since the Vassall house and possessions had been confiscated, she lived instead with her daughter's family in Boston. There she was beseiged by demands of payment by her late husband's creditors. Other relatives soon came to her rescue. Joseph Royall, an exile in London, gave her property in Dorchester and Milton, which she sold in several separate lots. Thomas Oliver, also in England, revived the West Indies plantation and leased it from the widow. This provided her a reliable income until her death in 1800. She is buried in the Vassall tomb in Christ Church.

Recent conservation reveals that the face and upper neck of this portrait are original; the sides and lower part of the painting are later additions.

Inventory of the Real & Personall Estate belonging to the ~~Estate of~~ Henry Vassall late of Cambridge Esq Deceas'd –

House Land Stable &c ... £ 1000

In the Best Room

In the Closett

In the Boffatt

In the Blue Room

In the Closett

In the Boffatt

In the Sleeping Room

In the Closett

In the Little Entry

In the Little Room

In the Kitchen

67A

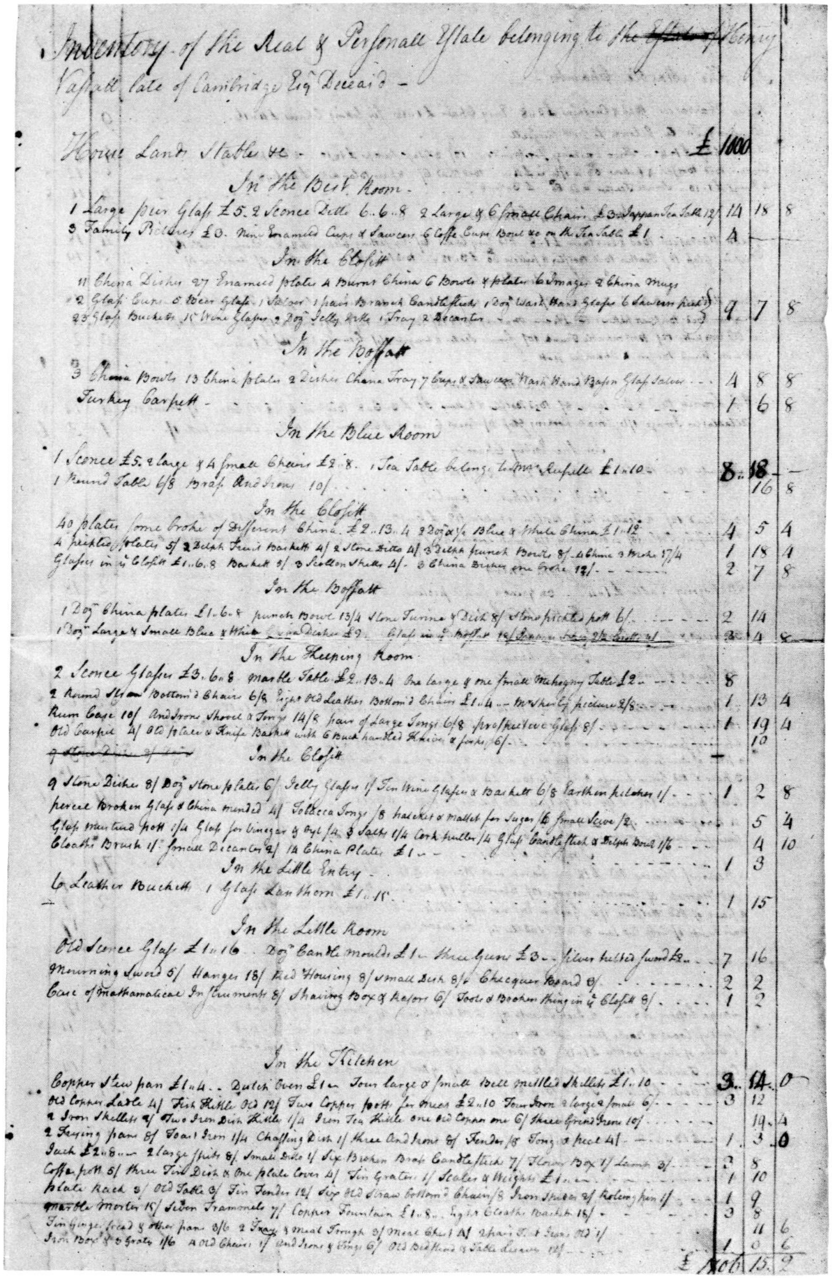

67A. **Inventory,** 1769

Photographic reproduction. H. 35.4 x 28 cm.

B. **Inventory,** 1778-79

Photographic reproduction. H. 35.4 x 28 cm.
Originals in the Middlesex County Probate Files, Cambridge, Massachusetts (Old Series, Nos. 23336 and 23342)

A comparison of two inventories of the Henry Vassall House provides us with a vivid example of the vicissitudes of Cambridge Loyalist life.

The first was taken on 8 September 1769, following Henry Vassall's death. As Samuel Batchelder has pointed out, the inventory represents only a portion of the original estate, which had once been so well provisioned that it had boasted its own fire engine. At his death, Vassall was bankrupt, having gone through most of his and his wife's properties. This inventory includes all of Vassall's remaining possessions — his house and lands, 150 pictures, more than 300 books, five slaves, several dogs, horses, and chariots — and places their value at over £4,000.

Since the widow Penelope Royall Vassall had been declared an "absentee" Loyalist who had "fled from her Habitation to the Enemies of this State," her property was confiscated and inventoried in preparation for its auction, which took place on 1 April 1779. One brief look at this inventory, taken by several Cambridge men on 24 June 1778, tells us the sad decline of the estate, which now totalled less than £200. The committee placed the greatest value on the one remaining chariot (£101) and the least on Tony, the Negro slave (£1).

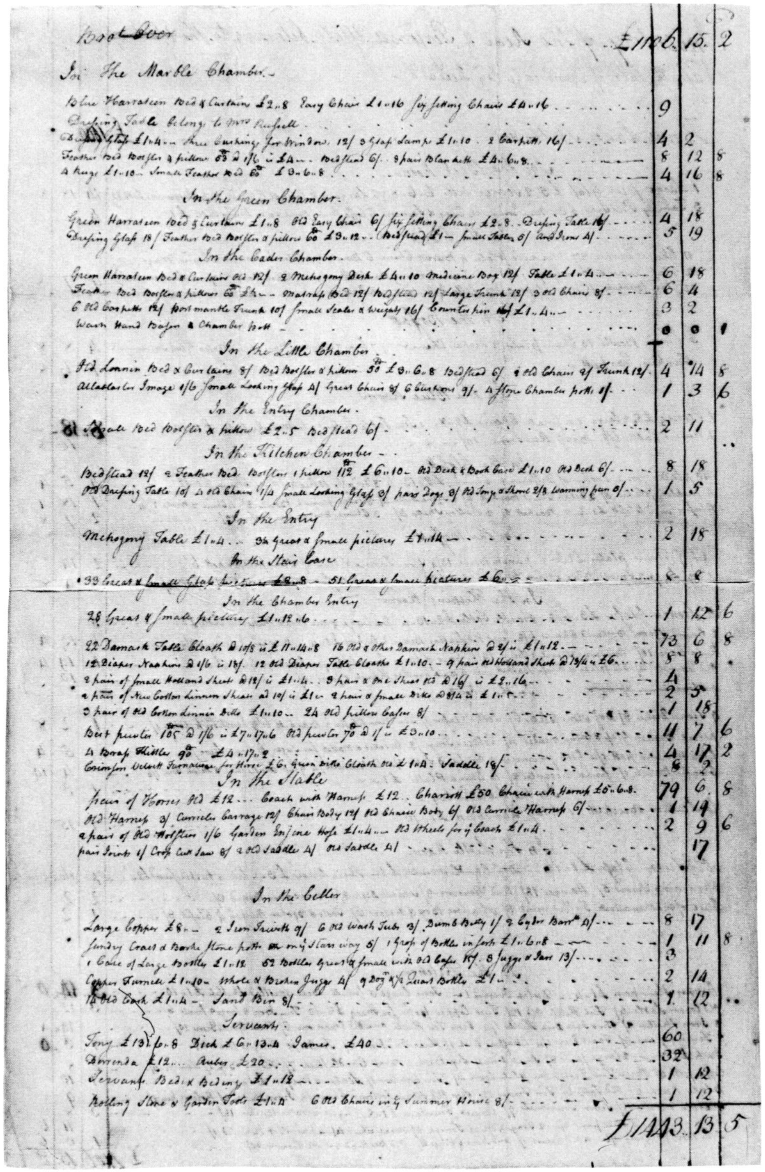

Brot Over £1106. 15. 2

In The Marble Chamber.

In the Green Chamber.

In the Cedar Chamber.

In the Little Chamber.

In the Entry Chamber.

In the Kitchen Chamber.

In the Entry.

In the Stair Case.

In the Chamber Entry.

In the Stable.

In the Cellar.

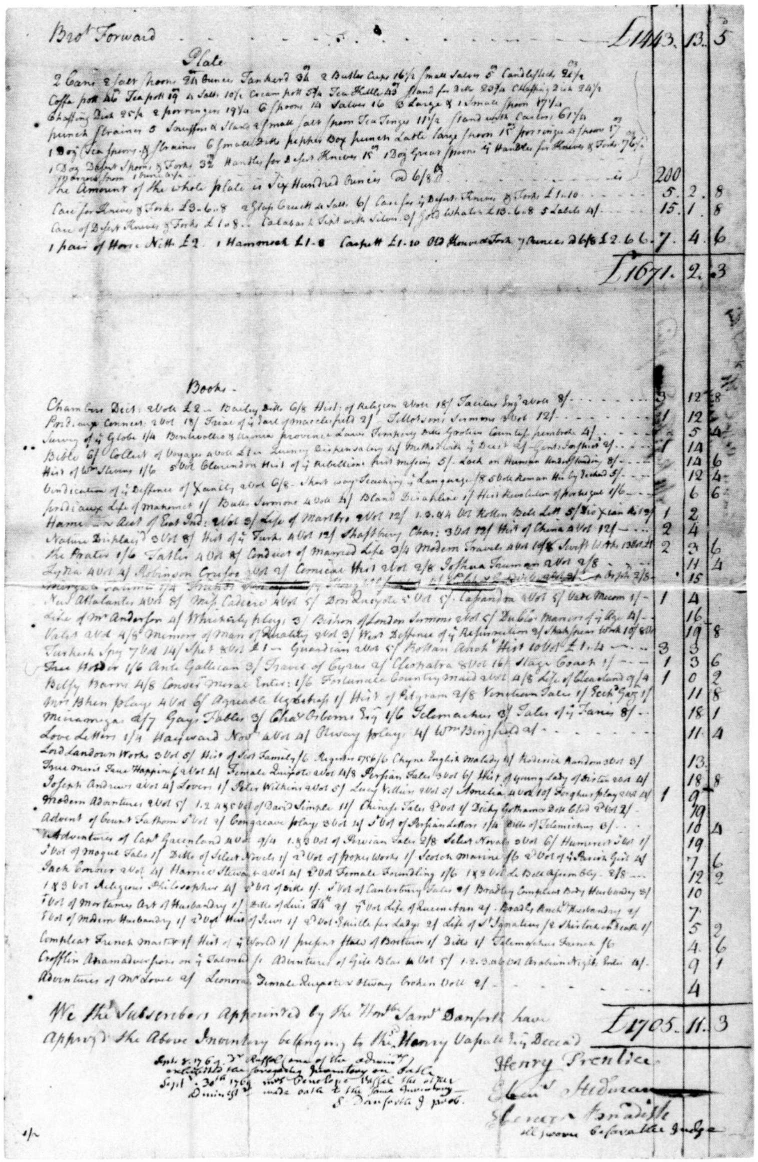

Servants.

£1193. 13. 5

Brot Forward £1443. 13. 5

Plate

£1671. 2. 3

Books.

We the Subscribers Appointed by the Honble Saml Danforth have Approvd the Above Inventory belonging to Mr Henry Vassall &c Deced

£1705. 11. 3

Henry Prentice

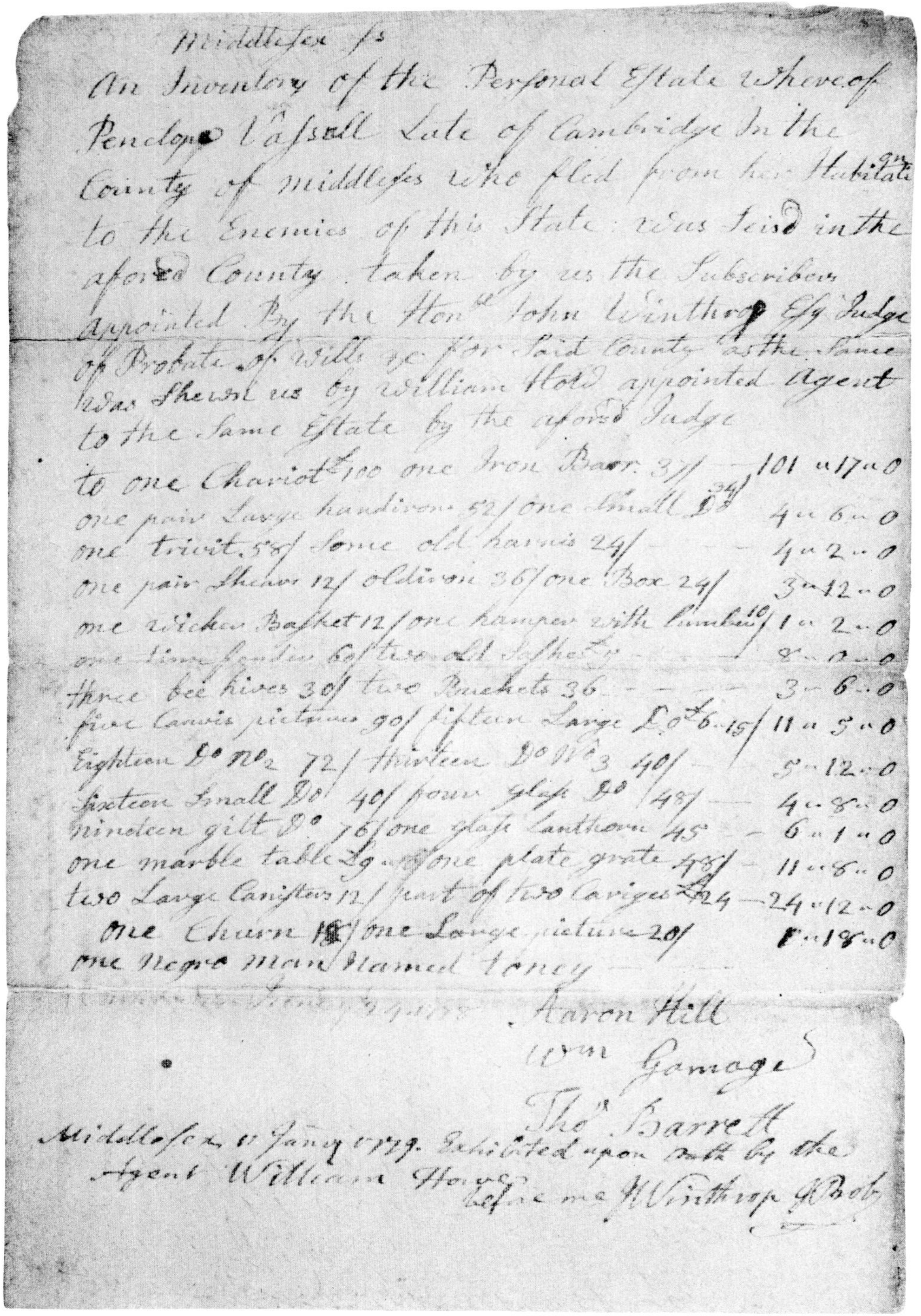

Middlesex ſs

An Inventory of the Perſonal Eſtate whereof
Penelope Vaſſall Late of Cambridge In the
County of Middleſex who fled from her Habitation
to the Enemies of this State: was ſeiz'd in the
aforeſd County, taken by us the Subscribers
appointed By the Honble John Winthrop Eſq Judge
of Probate & Wills &c for ſaid County as the ſame
was ſhewed us by William Hoſd appointed Agent
to the ſame Eſtate by the aforeſd Judge

to one Chariot 100 one Iron Barr. 3/	—	101 " 17 " 0
one pair Large handirons 52/ one ſmall 34		4 " 6 " 0
one trivit 5/ ſome old harnis 24/ —		4 " 2 " 0
one pair ſhears 12/ old iron 36/ one Box 24/		3 " 12 " 0
one wicker Basket 12/ one hamper with Lumber 10/		1 " 2 " 0
one lime ſeive 6/ two old ſhelfs 2/ —		8 " 0
three bee hives 30/ two Buckets 36 — —		3 " 6 " 0
five Canvis pictures 90/ fifteen Large Do Fº 15/		11 " 5 " 0
Eighteen Do Nº 2 72/ thirteen Do Nº 3 40/		5 " 12 " 0
ſixteen ſmall Do 40/ four glaſs Do 48/ —		4 " 8 " 0
nineteen gilt Do 96/ one glaſs Lanthorn 45		6 " 1 " 0
one marble table 9/ one plate grate 48/ —		11 " 8 " 0
two Large Canisters 12/ part of two Cavieres 24/		24 " 12 " 0
one Churn 16/ one Large picture 2/		8 " 18 " 0
one Negro man named Toney —		

Aaron Hill
Wm Gamage
Thos Barrett

Middleſex 11 Jany 1779 Exhibited upon oath by the
Agent William Hoſſe before me Winthrop J. Prob.

68. Henry Vassall House, November 1975

Photograph. H. 28 x 35 cm.
Paul Birnbaum, photographer

John Vassall, Sr. (A.B. 1732) bought this house and seven acres of land from Mercy Frizell for £1,000 in 1737. In 1741 he sold the property, including the barn and horses, outhouses, furniture, and chariot, to his young brother, Henry (cat. no. 65).

Until Henry's death in 1769, the house at 94 Brattle Street was the scene of grand picnics, concerts, dances, and gambling parties hosted by Vassall and his wife Penelope (cat. no. 66). A hedge of one hundred tall acacia trees gave the large estate more privacy. The garden was filled with fruit trees brought from England and France.

Later, the house, which had a "medicine-chest" reportedly large enough to supply a pharmacy, became the medical headquarters for the Continental Army. It was there that Dr. Benjamin Church, its surgeon-general, was arrested and imprisoned for corresponding with the British.

The Committee of Safety then seized the house and leased it for a small sum (due to its poor condition) to Capt. Nathan Adams of Charlestown. When the Convention troops, who had surrendered at Saratoga, were in Cambridge in 1777/78 awaiting transport from Boston to England, Adams housed General Burgoyne's staff officers there.

Massachusetts ordered the sale of this and other Loyalist estates in 1779. The property went first to the son of one of Henry Vassall's many creditors, who sold it to Nathaniel Tracy (cat. no. 71), who later sold it to Andrew Craigie. Neither of these men lived in the house, preferring instead the more formal and elegant house that Henry's nephew, Maj. John Vassall, had built across the street.

69. WARNER, William (1795-1830), American

Craigie House, 1815

Ink and watercolor on white wove paper. Image: H. 26 x 40.7 cm.; sheet: H. 72.5 x 53.4 cm.
Inscribed, below image: A PERSPECTIVE REPRESENTATION / OF / MR. CRAIGIES HOUSE. / WILLIAM A. WARNER. / 1815
Lent by Harvard University Archives (HUC 8815.593pf)

Maj. John Vassall, Jr. (A.B. 1757), heir to a large fortune, built this Georgian mansion in 1759, across Brattle Street from that of his uncle, Col. Henry Vassall (cat. no. 65). Although Vassall lived most of the year in his home on Tremont Street in Boston, he, like many other men of wealth, used his Cambridge estate (eighty-seven acres) as a summer home.

Vassall, like most of his family and friends, was a Loyalist. In 1774 he was named to the Mandamus Council (although never sworn in) and then was driven from his Cambridge home by "the intolerable threats and insolent treatment of mobs."[1] He first fled to Boston, and then to Halifax. Finally, on 12 May 1776, he sailed for England with his brother-in-law, Lt. Gov. Thomas Oliver (see cat. no. 72), and other prominent Cambridge Loyalists. In London Vassall lived comfortably among the exiled Massachusetts aristocrats, on a substantial income from his Jamaican plantations.

The Committee of Safety took over the Vassall House and used it as an army hospital and as quarters for a regiment of soldiers. On 15 July 1775 Gen. George Washington moved into the mansion, and from that time until the evacuation of Boston it served as the headquarters of the American Army. In December 1775 Martha Washington joined her husband, arriving in Cambridge in a coach with four black horses, postillions, and Negro servants dressed in scarlet and white livery. Washington remained in the house until the following spring.

The house and property were confiscated, and Vassall proscribed, in 1779. The house remained unoccupied until

June 1781 when Nathaniel Tracy (cat. no. 71), the first of several speculators to live there in luxury, bought the mansion and land for £4,264. Tracy lost his money and sold the house in 1786 to the Boston merchant Thomas Russell. By 1793 it was owned by Andrew Craigie. He was apothecary general during the Revolution and made a fortune in currency speculation. After the war, he speculated in real estate, developing Cambridge Street and Lechmere Point, now East Cambridge, and building Craigie's Bridge over the canal. He died bankrupt in 1819. After his death, Craigie's widow rented rooms in the John Vassall House to Harvard students, among them Josiah Quincy III, Edward Everett, and Jared Sparks — all future presidents of the College — and to Henry Wadsworth Longfellow, who arrived in 1837 as Professor of Modern Languages. In 1841, Nathan Appleton purchased the house, presenting it as a wedding gift to his daughter and Longfellow in 1843.

This mathematical thesis, drawn by a student named William Warner, shows the house as it must have looked right after Appleton bought it, with the side "piazzas" added during Craigie's ownership. Andrew Craigie not only enlarged the house but expanded the grounds, on which he built a greenhouse and summerhouse. By the time the Longfellows took possession, however, most of the land had been sold off in lots, and only about five acres remained. The Vassall-Craigie-Longfellow House is now a National Historic Site, under the jurisdiction of the National Park Service, Department of the Interior.

---

1. *Sibley's,* 14:231.

70A. Attributed to HURD, Nathaniel (1730-1777), American

Bookplate

Line engraving on paper. H. 10.6 x 8.4 cm.

B. Artist Unknown

Bookplate

Line engraving on paper. H. 9.6 x 7.2 cm.
Lent by the American Antiquarian Society

New England's prominent families carried on the tradition of using heraldry to ornament their bookplates, silver, and carriages. Usually, the coat of arms was displayed with the family motto.

Maj. John Vassall, to whom these bookplates belonged, expressed loyalty to King George III by dropping his family motto: *Saepe pro rege, semper pro republica* (Often for the king, always for the commonwealth). In the revised version of his bookplate, he also added a British flag to the ship at the crest.

Nathaniel Hurd, a silversmith and engraver, was the principal bookplate artist in pre-revolutionary Boston. The Vassall bookplate illustrates Hurd's skill with the Chippendale style, so called because of its affinity to the ornate, flowery work being produced in England by the cabinet-maker Thomas Chippendale.

The family coat of arms was a play on the name Vassall, featuring a goblet (vase or väs) under the sun (sol). The escutcheon on which the armorial bearings appear is mantled with elaborate convolutions, intertwined with delicate garlands of roses. A ship, perhaps symbolizing the Vassall family's merchant trade in the West Indies, serves as the crest. Vassall's name is boldly engraved on the bottom of the bookplate.

71. BROWN, Mather (1761-1831), American

Nathaniel Tracy (1751-1796), ca. 1785

Oil on canvas. H. 91.5 x 70 cm.
Provenance: Gen. William Raymond Lee of Boston, grandson of the sitter
Lent by the Newburyport Public Library, Newburyport, Massachusetts

One of the great financiers of the revolutionary era was Nathaniel Tracy (A.B. 1769), a Newburyport merchant. An ardent Patriot, Tracy donated large sums of money to clothe and feed the soldiers and poor during the war. He was a member of the Committee of Correspondence, "commissary of the sea coast forces," a backer of the Arnold expedition against Quebec, and owner of the first American privateer used against the British. He also served in the Massachusetts House and Senate and in 1782 was appointed justice of the peace.

Tracy collected luxurious country homes along the east coast of America. It is said he could travel from Newburyport to Virginia, sleeping in a house of his own every night.[1] In 1781 he added two more jewels to his collection — the once grand estates of Col. Henry Vassall and Maj. John Vassall in Cambridge.

As the war continued, most of Tracy's fleet was either captured or destroyed, and his business began to falter. He learned in 1785, upon return from a trip to Europe, that his property had been attached for debt. Bankrupt, he retired to his farmhouse in Newbury, where he spent the last ten years of his life.

Mather Brown was the son of Boston clockmaker Gawen Brown and his second wife Elizabeth Byles. For a short time, in 1775, he was a pupil of Gilbert Stuart who was in Boston awaiting transport to England. Hoping to raise enough money to follow Stuart to London, Brown left home and became an itinerant painter of miniatures. He finally sailed for London in 1780, equipped with letters of introduction from his grandfather, Rev. Mather Byles (cat. no. 20), addressed to Benjamin Franklin and "To Mr. Copley in the Solar System."

Young Mather's first letter from London in 1781 reported that the introductions had proved most helpful.

> In consequence of the recommendation of Dr. Franklin, who gave me letters to his fellow townsman, the famous Mr. West of Philadelphia, I practice gratis with this gentleman, who affords me every encouragement, as well as Mr. Copley, who is particularly kind to me, welcomed me to his home, and lent me his pictures, etc. . . .[2]

After studying with Benjamin West, Brown became sufficiently successful by 1784 to move into a fashionable house on Cavendish Square, where the English artist Romney had lived. He received commissions for portraits of the royal family and of such distinguished Americans as John Adams and Thomas Jefferson, as well as for history paintings. Mather Brown died in London in 1831.

1. *Sibley's*, vol. 17, forthcoming.
2. James H. Stark, *Loyalists of Massachusetts*, p. 280.

72. **Elmwood**, July 1974

Photograph. H. 28 x 35 cm.
Paul Birnbaum, photographer

In 1766 Thomas Oliver (A.B. 1753), the son of a wealthy Antiguan planter, bought a hundred acres of land, with a view of the Charles River, on the outskirts of Cambridge. The following year he built there the three-story Georgian mansion which we know today as Elmwood. The site was chosen for its proximity to the estates of the family of Elizabeth Vassall, whom Oliver had married in 1760. Her aunts were the wives of Judge Joseph Lee, Richard Lechmere, John Borland, and Timothy Ruggles, who had all built grand houses along Brattle Street. Her uncle, Col. Henry Vassall (cat. no. 65) and her brother, Maj. John Vassall, Jr. (see cat. no. 69) also lived nearby.[1] Before the Revolution, this elite group gathered almost daily at each other's houses for lavish entertainments.

Oliver had studied law after college, but soon found he had to devote his attentions to the management of the West Indies estates bequeathed him by his grandfather and great-uncle. He did find time, however, to hold various offices at Christ Church and to serve as justice of the peace and judge of the Vice-Admiralty Court. His political involvement grew deeper when, in 1774, he was sworn in as lieutenant governor and president of the Mandamus Council.[2]

A heretofore popular and respected gentleman, Oliver became the target of the townspeople's resentment. On 2 September 1774 the lieutenant governor's house was surrounded by some four thousand people who demanded his resignation from the Council. He at first refused to resign, but the crowd grew more impatient. In Oliver's words, they

> began to press up to my windows, calling for vengeances against the foes of their Liberty. . . . I could hear them from a distance swearing they would have my blood. At

this time the distress of my wife and children, which I
heard in the next room, called up feelings . . . which I
confess I could not suppress. I found myself giving way,
and at that instant, Nature, ingenious in forming new
reasons, suggested to my mind the calamities which
would ensue if I did not comply.[3]

Oliver, criticized by General Gage for his conduct, des-
perately sought to explain his actions to Lord Dartmouth
and to obtain Dartmouth's "acquittal." Meanwhile, he
and his family moved to Boston, since they no longer felt
safe in Cambridge. Oliver continued to exercise his appointed office and, from the time General Gage sailed
for England in October 1775 until his own departure in
March 1776, he served as acting governor of Massachusetts.

Although Oliver was disappointed at the pension and
compensation awarded him by the British government, he
managed to live quite comfortably from the income from
his Antiguan estates. After his wife's death in 1779,
Thomas Oliver joined other Massachusetts Loyalists at
Bristol, where he lived until his death in 1815.

During the Revolution, Elmwood had been occupied
by Benedict Arnold and his Connecticut troops, used as a
hospital for the Bunker Hill victims, and as quarters for
some of General Burgoyne's officers. The house and property (ninety-six acres) were confiscated and sold at auction
in 1779 for £47,000 to Andrew Cabot of Salem. Cabot in
turn sold the estate in 1787 to Elbridge Gerry (A.B. 1762;
LL.D. 1810), signer of the Declaration of Independence,
member of Congress, governor of Massachusetts, and
vice president of the United States.[4] Gerry's widow sold
the house and ten acres of land in 1818 to Rev. Charles
Lowell whose son, Prof. James Russell Lowell, named it
Elmwood.

The Oliver-Gerry-Lowell House is unique among the
Tory Row mansions. Beautifully restored, it still retains
spacious grounds. After the house was acquired by the
University in the early 1960s, it served as the residence of

Harvard's dean of Faculty. It is now the official home of Harvard's president.

1. Oliver was twice John Vassall's brother-in-law. Vassall's sister, Elizabeth, married Oliver in 1760 and Vassall married Oliver's sister, Elizabeth, in 1761. He was also doubly related to the Henry Vassalls. Colonel Vassall was his wife's uncle, and Penelope Royall Vassall's mother was Oliver's grandmother.
2. Although many thought Thomas Oliver had been named accidentally instead of Peter Oliver, Thomas Hutchinson was aware that he could not appoint another relative to high office without increasing the tensions between Britain and her colonies.
3. Letter, Thomas Oliver to Lord Dartmouth, 3 September 1774. Colonial Office Papers, Public Records Office, London (CO5/769/98-, 02). I am grateful to Prof. Bernard Bailyn for calling this letter to my attention and providing me access to it on microfilm.
4. Gerrymander, the division of a state or county into election districts in an unnatural or unfair way, was derived from his name.

73. BOYD, William (1776-1800), American

House of Samuel Webber and Court House, 1795

Ink and watercolor on cream laid paper. H. 32.7 x 37.2 cm.
Inscribed, at top of leaf: A NORTH EAST VIEW / OF / THE HOUSE of SAMUEL WEBBER, A.A.S., and of The COURT HOUSE in Cambridge.; below image: By an actual Survey.; below margin: WILLIAM BOYD fecit.
Lent by Harvard University Archives (HUC 8796.509 pf)

The third Middlesex County Courthouse, built in 1758, was thirty feet wide and forty feet long. It was painted yellow, with a red door and a cupola on top. This building was the scene of many colonial legal battles, bringing to Cambridge such noted justices as Hutchinson and Lynde. It was on the steps of this courthouse, in 1774, that Judges Samuel Danforth and Joseph Lee stood before an angry mob and resigned their positions as mandamus councillors.

After the court moved to East Cambridge in 1816, this building continued to be used for town meetings. The Harvard Cooperative Society stands today on the site of the Old Court House.

A garden separated the Court House from the Samuel Webber House. Following his graduation from Harvard in 1784, Webber was a tutor in mathematics until his appointment as fourth Hollis Professor of Mathematics and Natural Philosophy in 1789. Webber lived in this house, owned by the College, until 1806 when he was named president of Harvard and moved into Wadsworth House. He was a man "without friends or enemies." His presidency, perhaps the "most colorless" in Harvard's history, lasted only four years, until his death in 1810.[1] Although Webber attempted to establish an astronomical observatory at the College, he is best remembered for the "erect declining sun-dial" he built for Massachusetts Hall, and for helping to settle the northeastern boundary of the United States.

By an actual survey

This building, also known as College House No. 2, later became the first home of the Harvard Law School. It was torn down in 1844.

William Boyd (A.B. 1796) submitted this view in 1795. Although he began to study medicine after graduation, he died of consumption in 1800, before completing his course.

---

1. Samuel Eliot Morison, *Three Centuries of Harvard*, p. 195.

74. Boston Gazette & Country Journal, No. 1012

Boston: 5 September 1774. H. 29 x 25 cm.
Lent by the Houghton Library (T News 51.11)

This issue, 5 September 1774, of the *Boston Gazette* chronicled the traumatic events that had recently occurred in Cambridge: the removal of the ammunition from the powder-house, the gathering of the alarmed townspeople from Cambridge, Boston, and Charlestown, and the confrontation between the mob and the Tory office-holders.

On these pages are printed the resignations of Judges Joseph Lee and Samuel Danforth, and Lieutenant Governor Thomas Oliver from the Mandamus Council. Danforth swore "not to be any way concerned as a member of the Council at any time hereafter," while Lee declared he would "give no further attendance" (p. 2). Although the mob forced Oliver to resign as president of the Council, they did not seem to mind his retaining the office of lieutenant governor, "the place he held constitutionally." Oliver continued to serve in this position as long as the British held Boston.

The mob not only obtained the councillors' resignations, but harassed the rest of the Loyalist aristocracy until they fled Cambridge. Frightened by threats and insults, they left their mansions on Tory Row, many never to return.

75. Attributed to FEKE, Robert (fl. 1741-1750), American

Thomas Fayerweather (1724?-1804?), ca. 1742

Oil on canvas. H. 92.5 x 73.7 cm.
Anonymous Loan

The eighteenth-century genealogical records of the Fayer-weather family are complex. About 1720 a son Thomas was born to both John and Jerusha (Groce) Fayerweather, and to Thomas and Hannah (Waldo) Fayerweather.[1] One of these Thomases lived in the Fayerweather house on Brattle Street. Again confusingly, he has been described as "an ardent Whig," and "arbitrationist," and a Tory — perhaps because he seems not to have had strong leanings toward either side during the Revolution. He was not banished, nor did he lose any property, but he did live in seclusion in Oxford, Massachusetts during the Revolution.[2]

If Thomas's parents were indeed Thomas and Hannah Fayerweather, he would have been the brother of John Winthrop's wife, Hannah (1726-1790), who was a close friend of Mercy Otis Warren and Abigail Adams. His brother would have been Samuel Fayerweather (1724-1781; A.B. 1743), an Anglican minister.

1. The latter Thomas's dates are 1720-1805.
2. Mabel M. Swan, "Furniture of the Boston Tories," p. 189.

76. Attributed to FEKE, Robert (fl. 1741-1750), American

Sarah Hubbard (Mrs. Thomas Fayerweather, 1730-1804), ca. 1742

Oil on canvas. H. 90 x 72 cm.
Anonymous Loan

Sarah Hubbard was the daughter of Thomas Hubbard (1702-1773; A.B. 1721), who was the treasurer of Harvard College from 1750 until 1773. Sarah married Thomas Fayerweather in Boston on 24 June 1756.

Comparison of these two portraits to works by Robert Feke — *Isaac Royall and his Family,* in particular — have led Dr. Peter Mooz to attribute these paintings to that artist.[1]

---

1. I would like to thank Dr. R. Peter Mooz for allowing me to read his unpublished manuscript for an article which discusses the Fayerweather portraits.

77. HODGES, Benjamin (1785-1804), American

Fayerweather House, 1803

Watercolor and ink on white antique laid paper. H. 54 x 74.1 cm., irregular

Inscribed, u.c.: PERSPECTIVE VIEW of the HOUSE of MR FAYER-WEATHER / in CAMBRIDGE.; u.l.: A south east view taken according / to the rules of Perspective; u.r.: A south east view as corrected by the Camera Obscura; l.c.: To SAMUEL WEBBER, A.M.A.A.S. Professor of Mathematics &c. / Respectfully inscribed; l.l.: Harvard University April 26th 1803; l.r.: by Benjª Hodges, student.

Lent by Harvard University Archives (HUC 8803.539pf)

This house at 175 Brattle Street once stood in a large garden with forty-five acres of land stretching toward Fresh Pond. The large, three-story home was built in the early 1760s by Amos Marrett, who later became a Lexington Minuteman. Marrett sold the house, in 1771, to Col. George Ruggles, a Jamaican planter who had married Susanna Vassall (sister of Col. Henry; cat. no. 65). A Tory, Ruggles left Cambridge in 1774 after selling the house to Thomas Fayerweather (cat. no. 75) for £2000. Fayerweather owned it until his death in the early nineteenth century. After the battle of Bunker Hill, part of the house was used as a hospital.

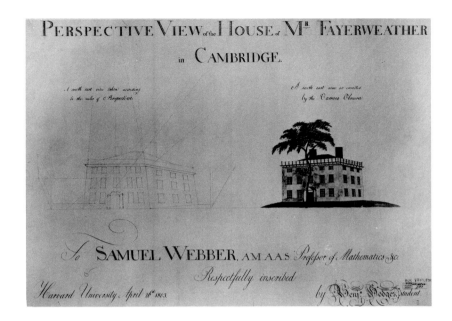

78. Hicks House, November 1975

Photograph. H. 28 x 35 cm.
Paul Birnbaum, photographer

The grand houses on Tory Row were not typical of those in which the majority of the townspeople lived. The Hicks House is more representative of the Cambridge home during the revolutionary era.

John Hicks, a carpenter, purchased part of his father's land on Dunster Street in 1760. Two years later, he built a six-room house with a large central chimney. The Hicks family, like so many others, was divided in its attitudes toward the Revolution. John Hicks was an ardent Patriot. His son, John, Jr., was a Tory and co-publisher of the *Massachusetts Gazette and Boston Post-Boy*. He fled to Halifax. Another son, Jonathan (A.B. 1770), became a surgeon in the revolutionary army.

John Hicks, Sr. was one of the first casualties of the War for Independence. Hearing about the fighting at Lexington and Concord, he rode to North Cambridge in hopes of meeting the retreating British soldiers. He and two other Cambridge men were killed by the British in the area of the present Massachusetts and Rindge Avenues. The men were quickly buried in a common grave in the yard of Christ Church.

Mrs. Hicks moved to a smaller house on Winthrop Street and, later that year, her former Dunster Street home was used as quarters for some of Washington's officers and as storage for supplies. The Hicks House had been seized earlier, in 1773, due to the elder Hicks's failure to settle his accounts as town tax collector. A friend, John Foxcroft, had bought the house and the Hicks family remained, probably as tenants.[1] The building was sold in 1903 to Harvard College and moved in 1928 to its present location at the corner of Boylston and South Streets. The building is now used as a library for Kirkland House.

1. Esther Stevens Fraser, "The John Hicks House," pp. 115-18.

79. FARRAR, Samuel (1773-1840), American

A Perspective View of the Episcopal Church, 1793

Ink and watercolor on cream antique laid paper. H. 36.1 x 43.5 cm.
Inscribed, within circles, in u.l.: A/Perspective / VIEW; u.r.: of /
the Episcopal CHURCH; l.l.: in Cambridge; l.r.: by / Saml Farrar. / 1793.
Lent by Harvard University Archives (HUC 8793.526pf)

On 5 April 1759 a group of prominent Cambridge men
wrote to London, petitioning the Society for the Propagation of the Gospel in Foreign Parts for the establishment
of an Anglican mission in Cambridge. The letter, sent to
Rev. Dr. Bearcroft, Secretary of the S.P.G., listed the reasons why the church was needed:

> . . . There is no Church nearer to us than Boston, which
> is from some of us eight, from others ten or twelve miles
> distant; unless, for shortening the way we submit to the
> inconvenience of crossing a large ferry, which in stormy
> weather, and in the winter season, especially, is very
> troublesome and sometimes impracticable. The Society
> will easily conceive the difficulty of conveying whole
> families to a place of public worship at such a distance,
> and attended by such obstructions. To remedy which, we
> have agreed to build a Church at Cambridge, which, as
> it is in the center, may indifferently serve the neighboring
> places, of Charlestown, Watertown, and Newtowne; be-
> sides providing for the young Gentlemen who are stu-
> dents at the College here, many of whom, as they have
> been brought up in the Church of England, are desirous
> of attending the worship of it. . . .[1]

Two years after the request was granted, on 15 October
1761, opening services were held in Christ Church near
Cambridge Common.

Christ Church's architect was Peter Harrison (1716-
1775; see below), designer of King's Chapel in Boston,
where the Cambridge Anglicans had worshipped previously. The plan and detail of the two churches are quite
similar.

A building committee headed by Henry Vassall chose
Harrison, a Newport resident, for the job, selected part

of the Common and part of the James Read estate for the site, and set down specific instructions: the church should be made of wood, with a covering of "rough-cast"; there should be a tower with belfry, but no steeple; the dimensions should be sixty feet long and forty-five feet wide; and the cost should not exceed £500. Since the costs rose to £1300, the building was never "rough-cast," nor were the pillars or capitals carved.

Most of the materials for the building came by water, up the Charles River to the Common. Nails and window glass came from England, and stone ballast was purchased from ships for the construction.[3]

The S.P.G.'s first minister to Cambridge, East Apthorp (cat. no. 14), became embroiled in a heated controversy and withdrew to England after only three years. His successor, Samuel Griffith, lasted a year before being sent to prison for fraud and theft.

It was not until June 1767 that a new minister, Winwood Serjeant, came to Christ Church and things at long last quieted down for the small congregation. But the calm lasted scarcely seven years. Many of Christ Church's communicants were wealthy Loyalists and as the political situation deteriorated in the summer and fall of 1774, the majority fled Cambridge.

In 1775 the church became a barracks for Connecticut troops. Damage was inevitable, especially once the soldiers decided to melt down the available metal, including the organ pipes, into bullets.

A very special service, however, necessitated the partial repair of the battered chapel. On New Year's Eve, 1775, George Washington, with the general's officers, staff, and their wives and families, attended the service at Christ Church. This was the last regular church service until 1790, when the building was restored.

America's first architect, Peter Harrison, was born to Quaker parents in York, England. Settling in Rhode Island in the late 1730s, Harrison used brains, ability, and a profitable marriage to establish himself as a prosperous gentleman merchant in partnership with his brother Joseph.

Within a decade after his arrival in the colonies, Peter Harrison had acquired proficiency in shipbuilding, cartography, surveying, military engineering, and drafting. He turned next to architecture, studying the works of William Kent and the earl of Burlington. His earliest commission, the Redwood Library in Newport, introduced the Palladian style to the colonies. He rarely received remuneration for his work, considering it a privilege and responsibility to serve his church (he had converted to Anglicanism) and the public.[4]

In 1766 Joseph Harrison was made a customs collector in Boston. This obliged him to relinquish the collectorship of New Haven, which he passed on to Peter. As an Anglican, a Tory, and a royal officer, Peter suffered increasing unpopularity in the last years before the Revolution. After his death in 1775, his mansion was plundered by a mob that destroyed his library and his drawings and architectural designs. Mrs. Harrison and her daughters fled to Newport, only to be harassed further there.

This watercolor, by Samuel Farrar, a Harvard student (A.B. 1793), shows the sturdy oak exterior painted gray with white trim and red doors, as it appears today.

---

1. Gardiner M. Day, *Biography of a Church*, pp. 2-3.
2. John Perkins Brown, "Christ Church, Cambridge," p. 18.
3. Carl Bridenbaugh, *Peter Harrison*, p. 114.
4. *Ibid.*, pp. 115-18. He was paid £45 in 1761 for drawing the plan for Christ Church.

80. GARTHORNE, Francis (fl. ca. 1677-1726), English

Communion Service, 1694

Silver. Flagon: H. 32 cm.; DIAM. base 17.2 cm. Cup with paten cover:
H. cup 21 cm.; DIAM. cover 13.4 cm.

Inscribed, under edge of foot of cup and flagon: The gift of K William & Q Mary to yᵉ Reveᵈ Samˡˡ Myles for yᵉ use of their Majᵗⁱᵉˢ Chappell in N:England:1694

Engraved, on flagon, cup, and cover: Royal Arms flanked with WM and R

Marks: on cover, and below rim of flagon; below rim of cup; inside paten cover: leopard's head crowned, black-letter r for 1694/95, lion passant, maker's mark FG with pellet below

Lent by Christ Church, Cambridge

It was customary for the crown, as head of the Church of England, to send gifts of silver, books, furniture, and linen to colonial churches through its governors. Following this tradition, William and Mary presented a large silver communion service in 1694 to Rev. Samuel Myles, rector of King's Chapel, Boston. It was used there until 1772 when a new governor, Thomas Hutchinson, received gifts of pulpit furniture and communion plate from George III. Hutchinson presented these to King's Chapel, where he worshipped, and divided the older communion service between Christ Church, Cambridge and St. Paul's, Newburyport.

Christ Church received three of the thin, hand-wrought silver pieces: a flagon, a cup, and a paten. The flagon consists of a plain cylinder that broadens into a splayed foot; the flat-topped lid with thumbpiece is hinged to an S-shaped handle. The bell-shaped chalice is also unornamented, save for the royal arms and monogram. Its stem, shaped like a spool, supports the cup and leads to a splayed foot. The paten, which fits as a cover on top of the chalice, has a base that can also be used as a handle.[1]

The communion service is the work of the English silversmith Francis Garthorne, who worked at the sign of the Sun in Swithin's Lane.

Christ Church still uses the communion service for its Christmas and Easter celebrations.

---

1. E. Alfred Jones, *The Old Silver of American Churches*, pp. 110-11.

81. PAINE, Robert (1770-1798)

Fourth Meetinghouse of the First Church, a View of the Left Side, 1788

Pencil drawing, with wash, pen, and ink on white laid paper.
  H. 35.3 x 40.6 cm.
Watermark: J. Whatman & Co.
Inscribed, in wreath, u.l.: The height of Cam- / bridge meeting house, / by Robert Paine, / being 130 feet. Octo- / ber th 2d 1788.; in pencil, under wreath, in a later hand: Robert Paine Esq. died July 1798 / of Yellow Fever. H.C. '89.; on back: The Gift of R.T. Paine Esq. of Boston. Rec d Aug. 3d. 1842.
Lent by Harvard University Archives; gift of Robert Treat Paine, 1842 (HUV 2188pf)

In November 1753 the town of Cambridge voted to build a new meetinghouse for the use of its Congregational residents, which included most of the town, and of Harvard College. On 3 December that year the Harvard Corporation voted to pay "one seventh part of the charge of said house," provided that the entire front gallery be reserved for the students and the president be given his choice of the third and fourth pew.[1]

Negotiations then began regarding the location of the building. In order to "secure it from fire as well as render the appearance of it much more beautiful" the town wanted to erect the meetinghouse farther back from the street than the previous building. The parish requested access to part of the president's orchard so that when worshippers "came to attend on divine worship they might place their horses, chairs, chaises, &c."[2] The Corporation voted on 6 September 1756 to allow the parish the use of this land, but set down more specific conditions, including a stipulation that the building face south and that the president be allowed "to cart into his back yard, viz., at the backside of the said new meeting house, wood, hay, boards, &c., for his own or the College use, as there shall be occasion for it."[3]

The fourth meetinghouse of the First Congregational

Church was finally raised on 17 November 1756, and the first service held the following week. The cost for the building (ca. seventy-five feet long and fifty feet wide) was approximately £1,500, with the College paying its share of £213 6s. 8d.

The ground floor was divided into square pews, with hinged seats which were raised to allow room for standing during prayers. There was no organ, but music was provided by a volunteer choir, accompanied by bass viol and a few wind instruments.

This meetinghouse was the focus of the town's activities during most of the eighteenth century. Harvard students and faculty attended compulsory services here until 1814.[4] As the largest auditorium in town, it was the scene of commencements and inaugurations. While the provincial troops were in Cambridge, George Washington and his staff worshipped there. The Provincial Congress met there twice in 1774, to elect its committees of safety and supplies. And it was in this building, in 1779, that the delegates from the province's towns met to frame the constitution of the Commonwealth of Massachusetts.

In 1833 the meetinghouse was torn down, and the land where it stood (the site of the present Lehmann Hall), the parsonage, and its lot were sold to Harvard. The College, in return, built the church which still stands on the corner of Massachusetts Avenue and Church Street, across from Harvard Yard.

This view of the First Church's fourth meetinghouse was prepared as a mathematical thesis for the Exhibition (held at the semi-annual meeting of the Harvard Overseers) of October 1788. It was drawn by Robert Paine (A.B. 1789), the eldest son of Robert Treat Paine (A.B. 1749) who signed the Declaration of Independence. The younger Paine died in 1798, after only a few years of law practice.

1. Paige, *History of Cambridge*, 1:291.
2. *Ibid.*
3. *Ibid.*, p. 292.
4. Even during the twenty-year period in which Holden Chapel was used for daily prayers, the Harvard community continued to meet on Sunday at the Congregational meetinghouse (Morison, *Three Centuries*, p. 94).

82. COPLEY, John Singleton (1738-1815), American

Rev. Nathaniel Appleton (1693-1784), ca. 1759-61

Oil on canvas. H. 90.5 x 74.8 cm.
Inscribed, on title band of book: Orth/&/Char.
Provenance: John James Appleton, great grandson of the sitter
Harvard University Portrait Collection; left in the keeping of Harvard College by John James Appleton in 1855 (H 19)

Nathaniel Appleton (A.B. 1712) had strong ties with Harvard College. He was related to three presidents. Through his mother, he was the grandson of John Rogers and the nephew of John Leverett. Edward Holyoke, whose portrait by Copley is similar in style to this one, was his brother-in-law.

As pastor of the First Church in Cambridge, Rev. Nathaniel Appleton was an *ex officio* member of the Harvard Corporation for sixty-one years, a record for Harvard officers.[1] Most of the students attended his services at the Cambridge meetinghouse, and he was extremely popular with them.

In 1771 Harvard honored him with the degree of Doctor of Sacred Theology (S.T.D.). It had been awarded only once before, to Increase Mather in 1692. The Corporation voted that Appleton had been

> long an ornament to the pastoral character and eminently distinguished for his knowledge Wisdom Sanctity of manners and usefulness to the Churches — and having for more than fifty Years exerted himself in promoting the Interests of Piety & learning in this Society . . .[2]

At his death in 1784, he left £30 to Harvard for the establishment of a scholarship, which is still awarded annually.

Like most Congregational ministers, Nathaniel Appleton was a Patriot. He persuaded many students to enlist in the Continental Army and himself served as chaplain to the First Revolutionary Provincial Congress.

The Reverend Dr. Appleton, shown here in clerical garb, is seated behind a table. In his right hand he holds a copy of Watt's *Orthodoxy and Charity*, the title of which was said also to have been his motto.

X-rays indicate that this painting has been repainted in several areas. The clerical collar has been altered and the lower section of the wig and face retouched. It was probably damaged and repainted late in the eighteenth century.[3]

---

1. *Sibley's,* 5:604.
2. *Ibid.,* 5:603.
3. Prown, *John Singleton Copley,* 1:34.

83. GREEN, Joshua, Jr. (1764-1847), American

Plot of Cambridge Common, ca. 1781

Watercolor and ink on cream antique laid paper. H. 46.7 x 65.3 cm.
Inscribed, in a scroll, l.r.: A Plot of / Cambridge Common / with a View of / the Roads, / & a principal part / of the Buildings / thereon / Contents / Ac[res]. R[oo]ds. P[er]ch[es]. Dec. [imal] Pt[s] / 15″01″00″ 3365.6.
Provenance: Dr. Samuel Abbott Green, grandson of the artist
Lent by Harvard University Archives; gift of Dr. S. A. Green (UAI.15.740pf)

When the town of Cambridge (then known as Newtowne) was founded in 1630, a large area of land was reserved for common use — for pasturing cattle, for elections, for militia training. During the Great Awakening, George Whitefield preached there. And every year, at Harvard commencement, the Common looked like a country fair, with tents and booths set up for refreshments and entertainment. Drinking, gambling (and sometimes rioting) made this a special holiday for the province.

In 1774 another form of rioting took place, as a mob of two thousand met and forced the town's mandamus councillors to resign.

One thousand men gathered at Cambridge Common on 16 June 1775 to march to Bunker Hill, and during the Revolution the Common became an army camp. Nine thousand men were quartered there in tents when George Washington arrived in July to take command and organize the troops. Later, barracks were built to house the soldiers.[1]

The survey of Cambridge Common was a favorite subject for the students' mathematical theses. Included in this view are individual perspective drawings of nearby buildings. In addition to the College (Holden Chapel, Hollis Hall, Harvard Hall, old Stoughton Hall, and Massachusetts Hall), we see Christ Church, the schoolhouse, a barn on the Prentice estate, the "Laboratory" or magazine re-

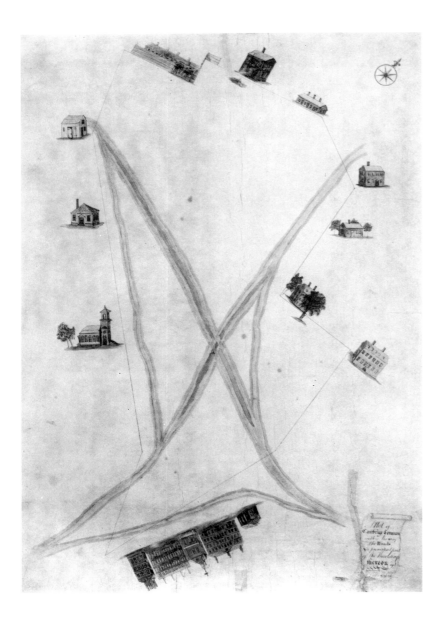

maining from the army barracks, the Waterhouse house, the blacksmith shop, John Nutting's house, another barn, John Hastings' house and the Jonathan Hastings house (where Oliver Wendell Holmes, Sr. was later born).[2]

This view was prepared by Joshua Green, Jr. A.B. 1784), the nephew of Ebenezer Storer (cat. no. 51). After graduation, he moved to Wendell, Massachusetts, where he served as selectman, justice of the peace, and representative. He died there in 1847.

---

1. After the soldiers left in 1776, the barracks were used as firewood by the townspeople, but the magazine and three cannon remained on the Common (Batchelder, *Bits of Harvard History*, pp. 255-57).
2. Hamilton Vaughan Bail, *Views of Harvard*, pp. 73-74.

84. BELL, D[aniel?]

View of Cambridge Common from the Seat of Caleb Gannett, ca. 1808-09

Watercolor on cream wove paper. H. 43.6 x 69.8 cm.
Inscribed, l.r.: Drawn by D. Bell; l.c.: Cambridge Common from Seat of Caleb Gannett, Esq! / Comprehending a view of Harvard University.
Provenance: Nehemiah Parsons; his daughter, Miss Anna Q. T. Parsons of Roxbury
Lent by Harvard University Archives (HUV 2208)

A later view of Cambridge Common was taken from the home of Caleb Gannett (A.B. 1763), who was first a tutor in mathematics at Harvard, and then long served as the College steward (1779-1818).

Although the College buildings can barely be seen behind the row of poplar trees, this watercolor gives us a good idea of Harvard Square at the turn of the century. To the right of Harvard is the Congregational meeting-house, Willard's Tavern (and several other buildings west of the Square), the cupola of the Middlesex County Courthouse, the hearse house and graveyard, the Brattle

House,[1] Christ Church, and a few houses along the Common.

Cambridge Common at this time was still unfenced, with several roads crossing through it. It extended from Waterhouse Street to Boylston Street, and included much of the present Harvard Square.[2] This view depicts the two main roads: the highway to Charlestown (now Kirkland St.) on the left; the road to Concord (Massachusetts Ave.) to the right.[3]

Gannett's house and estate were bought by the College in 1829 and the house torn down. A railroad station (later used as college commons) was soon built on the land. Today it is the site of the Harvard Law School.

1. Gannett's first wife was Gen. William Brattle's daughter; his second was the daughter of Ezra Stiles.
2. Charles Warren, *History of the Harvard Law School and of Early Legal Conditions in America*, 1:321.
3. Bail, *Views of Harvard*, p. 120.

*Cambridge Common from the Seat of Caleb Gannett Esqr.
Comprehending a view of Harvard University.*

V. The Hollis Family

The bequests of the Hollis family to Harvard College, which continued until 1804, began with an Englishman named Thorner in 1690. Robert Thorner, uncle of Thomas Hollis III, left £500 sterling to "Harvard College in New England whereof Mr. Increase Mather is now president." Thomas Hollis III (cat. nos. 85, 86) and his heirs were trustees of this bequest.

Thomas Hollis III was, like his father and grandfather, a prosperous London merchant and Dissenter, who regarded himself "as an almoner of providence, and his wealth as a trust." Thomas Hollis II had founded and supported two churches, two schools for the poor, and an almshouse, and sent books to Harvard College. After his death in 1718, his son retired from business and turned his attentions towards the little college in New England. Thomas III had earlier decided to bequeath Harvard £100 sterling, but now he determined to "act as his own executor." In the twelve years remaining to him he gave the College funds to support a professor of divinity, another of mathematics and natural philosophy, and ten scholars. He also sent books and scientific apparatus, and urged others to do so. He promoted the publication of the Harvard Library catalogue in 1723, so that he could better direct gifts to the College Library. He recruited men of note to aid the College, such as Isaac Watts and Daniel Neal, his own brothers Nathaniel and John, and his nephew and heir, Thomas Hollis IV. Nathaniel Hollis gave money for the education of two Indian boys and for the purchase of scientific instruments. John sent books worth £65 to Harvard in 1724. His son, Timothy, gave £20 for the restoration of the College Library after the fire. In 1732 Thomas IV sent the College £700, so that the Hollis Professors' salaries could be raised; plus an armillary sphere, an orrery, and a double microscope. The following year he sent a valuable collection of books. Between 1719 and 1733 the Hollis family sent to Harvard more than £3300 sterling in books, scientific apparatus and endowment funds.

Thomas III was a pious, though liberal, Baptist. He directed his bounty towards Harvard because he felt it to be the most liberal Protestant university of its time, more so than the English sectarian academies or the Anglican universities at Oxford and Cambridge. Benjamin Colman, the most cosmopolitan and catholic of Boston's clergymen, became his local contact. Hollis pressed Colman to accept the presidency of Harvard in 1724 and used him to repulse other supplicants for his bounty, most notably from the college in Connecticut and Rev. Thomas Prince's library in Boston. Hollis also aided the College privately in its English affairs but, as a retired gentleman, declined "the public show" attendant upon a more active role.

In the late 1730s Thomas Hollis V (cat. nos. 87-90), better known as Thomas Hollis of Lincoln's Inn, inherited the substantial estates of his father, grandfather and great-uncle. He abandoned his preparation for a mercantile career and instead began to fit himself for the life of a gentleman by studying at Gresham College in London and travelling for five years on the continent.

Like his ancestors, he was aware of the responsibility which his wealth conveyed. He returned to England with the intention of entering public life but could not countenance the corruption of Georgian politics. Instead he devoted his life to the preservation and extension of liberty throughout the world. He sent books to libraries in England, on the continent, and in America in a sophisticated propaganda campaign to make people aware of their liberties and of the need for constant vigilance in their defense. Above all, he sent the so-called "canonical books" of the radical Whig ideology, among them Harrington's *Commonwealth,* Sidney's *Discourses,* and Needham's *Excellencie of a Free State.* Such works were fundamental to a free society for, as he was fond of inscribing in his gift volumes, "If Government goeth right, ALL goeth right."

Hollis did not merely purchase books in order to donate them. He employed printers, etchers, engravers, and designers to produce new editions ornamented with engravings of his heroes, and bindings marked with symbolic devices which were in themselves a commentary on the text. In addition, he underlined and annotated many of the volumes, oftentimes copying favorite quotations into the margins or the flyleaves. In this way he became in the words of James Boswell, "the strenuous Whig, who used to send . . . presents of democratical books, with their boards stamped with daggers and caps of liberty."[1]

After 1764 the destruction of the Harvard Library by fire and his increasing pessimism about the fate of liberty in England led him to concentrate his philanthropic energies on Harvard. The growing American crisis increased his sense of urgency, as he shared with the colonists their fear of a ministerial plot against the liberties of Englishmen.

Attracted to Jonathan Mayhew by his inflammatory *Discourse Concerning Unlimited Submission*, Hollis made him his chief friend and agent in New England. Hollis labored mightily, until his retirement in 1770, to educate the Americans in the English tradition of resistance and to make the American cause known in England. He made the family relationship with Harvard, which had begun in an attempt to lead the College into an enlightened tolerant liberalism, into a powerful tool for political education.

Thomas Brand-Hollis (cat. no. 90), the heir to the fortune of Thomas Hollis V, continued the tradition of benefactions to Harvard College, donating a chest microscope and books.

The Hollis family interest in Harvard encompassed the entire eighteenth century. And, at two critical moments in the history of the College — the end of the Puritan period and the eve of the Revolution — the Hollises placed their influence on the side of the forces of change. Although no Hollis ever set foot in America, the family contributed greatly to the development of eighteenth-century Harvard.

---

1. William Bond, "Assertor of Liberty, Citizen of the World," p. 34.

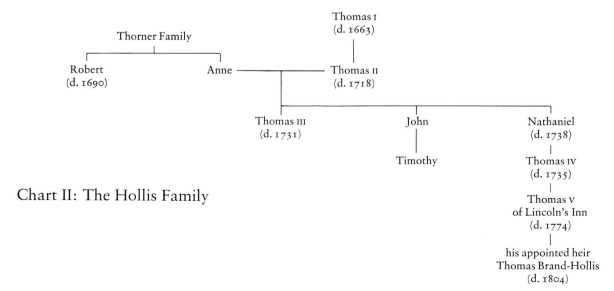

Chart II: The Hollis Family

85. PELHAM, Peter (ca. 1697-1751), English, after Joseph
   Highmore (1692-1780), English

Thomas Hollis (1660-1731), 1751

Mezzotint. Image: H. 30.2 x 24.9 cm.; image with lettering: H. 35 x 25
   cm.; sheet: H. 35.6 x 25.7 cm.; irregular. Plate mark indiscernible
Inscribed, across lower margin: Thomas Hollis late of London
   Merch.t a most generous Benefactor / to Harvard College, in N.E.
   having founded two Professorships and ten / Scholarships in the
   said College, given a fine Apparatus for Experimental / Phil-
   osophy, & increased the Library with a large Number of valuable
   Books &c.
Inscribed, l.l.: Jos. Highmore pinx. 1722; l.c.: Ob: 1731. Æ!71.;
   l.r.: P. Pelham ab Origin: fecit et excudt 1751.
Fogg Art Museum, Print Department; bequest of Boylston A. Beal
   (M 13,349)

Thomas Hollis III, a retired hardware merchant, began
his donations to Harvard College in 1719, when he was
nearly sixty years of age. From that time until his death
in 1731, "scarcely a ship sailed from London . . . without
bearing some evidence of his affection and liberality."[1] In
1719 he sent books for the library "for the assistance of
pious young men, who were destined for the ministry."
He also sent nails, cutlery, and arms, all of which were
to be sold for the benefit of poor scholars. The proceeds
amounted to £300. The following year he sent an additional £700 for divinity scholarships and inquired how
his future gifts might best be expressed. Surprised to learn
that Harvard did not have a professor of divinity, Hollis,
in 1721, endowed the first professorial chair in America.

The Hollis Professor of Divinity, who would receive
forty pounds per annum for his lectures, could not be
disqualified "on account of his belief and practice of
adult baptism."[2] The first Hollis Professor, Edward Wigglesworth (A.B. 1710), was however, thoroughly questioned on the "soundness and orthodoxy" of his principles
by the Congregational Board of Overseers before being
appointed.

Although representatives from Yale tried to persuade

Thomas Hollis late of London Merch.a a most generous Benefactor
to Harvard College, in N.E having founded two Professorships and ten
Scholarships in the said College, given a fine Apparatus for Experimental
Philosophy, & increased the Library with a large Number of valuable Books &c.
Jos. Highmore pinx. 1722.   Ob.1731. Æ.71.   P.Pelham ab Origin: fecit et excud.t 1751

Hollis to turn his benefactions to the college at New Haven, he continued to send money and books to Harvard.

Hollis endowed the second professorial chair at Harvard — and in America — in 1727, with a gift of £1200 plus several pieces of scientific apparatus. The first Hollis Professor of Mathematics and Natural Philosophy was Isaac Greenwood, a man of dubious qualities, who was hastily elected by the Overseers, when Hollis threatened to send a Baptist to fill the post. He was dismissed in 1738 for drunkenness.

In 1722 President Leverett finally persuaded a reluctant Thomas Hollis III to allow Joseph Highmore to paint his portrait for the College.[3] This grand painting was sent to Cambridge, and hung on the second floor of Harvard Hall until destroyed in the fire of 1764. Fortunately, we have an idea of what the portrait was like from this mezzotint engraving by Peter Pelham, stepfather of John Singleton Copley.

In its meeting of 15 May 1751 the Corporation voted that:

> liberty be given to Mr. Pelham of Boston Painter to take a Mezzotinto Print from Mr. Hollis's Picture now standing in the Hall; Provided All due Care be taken by him that no Injury be done to s'd Picture.[4]

By September the print was ready to be issued and was advertised in the *Boston Newsletter* (17 September 1751) as follows:

> To be sold, at his home near the Quaker Meeting House, a print in Metzotintu of Thomas Hollis late of London merchant, . . . done from a curious whole length Picture by Joseph Highmore in London, and Placed in the College Hall in Cambridge.[5]

Peter Pelham arrived in Boston in 1727, having received his training from the mezzotintist John Simon. In England, he had engraved works after Kneller, but in Boston, he found he had to first paint the portrait himself, before he could engrave it. This is the procedure he used to produce his portrait of *Cotton Mather*, believed to be the first mezzotint made in America. After John Smibert arrived in Boston, Pelham engraved six portraits after his paintings of popular New England figures. In comparison with Pelham's simple colonial portraits, this engraving of Hollis is closer to the more sophisticated, elegant prints Pelham made while in England.

Pelham's mezzotints of military and religious leaders sold well. But he could not support his family from this trade, and actually became better known as a schoolmaster who taught reading, writing, dancing, needlework, music and painting to the children of Boston.[6] Mary Copley, after her marriage to Pelham in 1748, continued to run her late husband's tobacco shop in order to bring in additional income for the family.

It is likely that Peter Pelham gave John Singleton Copley the only artistic training he was to receive. In 1753, at the age of fifteen, young Copley took his stepfather's copper plate for his portrait of Rev. William Cooper, made some changes, and issued his first and last mezzotint engraving, a portrait of Rev. William Welsteed.

---

1. Josiah Quincy, *The History of Harvard University*, 1:430.

2. *Ibid.*, p. 239.

3. Joseph Highmore was first apprenticed to an attorney, then trained in Kneller's art academy for ten years. By 1715 he was an established portrait painter. His rococo style appealed to the king, who commissioned him to make several portraits of members of the royal family. He was noted for his illustrations for Samuel Richardson's novels and for his conversation pieces. Highmore's portrait of Thomas Hollis at age seventy-one, with gilt frame, cost £28.

4. Anne Allison, "Notes on the Hollis Portraits," p. 2.

5. *Ibid.*

6. Andrew Oliver, "Peter Pelham (ca. 1697-1751) Sometime Printmaker of Boston," p. 149.

86. COPLEY, John Singleton (1738-1815), American

Thomas Hollis (1660-1731), 1766

Oil on canvas. H. 237 x 147 cm.
Inscribed, on letter on table: To the Rev•J•Leveret, President of Harvard Colledge in New England
Provenance: Commissioned from Copley by the Harvard Corporation, 1765/66
Harvard University Portrait Collection (H 25)

Following the fire of 1764, Thomas Hollis V asked Cipriani to paint a portrait of his great-uncle, Thomas Hollis III, taken after a life portrait that young Hollis owned. The Cipriani portrait, now part of the Harvard University Portrait Collection (H 83), was shipped to Harvard in August 1764.

The Harvard Corporation lent the Cipriani bust as a model to John Singleton Copley and asked him to paint a life-size portrait of the College's great benefactor. The Treasurer's Journal shows payment of £22 8s. to Copley on 14 July 1766.[1] Apparently unsatisfied with this sum, the artist refused to return the Cipriani. In an undated letter, President Holyoke told Copley that he and the Corporation thought "it would be quite improper to part with the Picture sent by Mr. Hollis — are willing to pay Mr. Copley for the other, but earnestly desire the small one be put up to be ready when the President shall send for it."[2] In another letter, dated 31 January 1767, Holyoke informed Copley that he was ready to send for the Cipriani, and added:

> . . . if you must have more for the new Picture, let it be so, and as for yor letting us have it Cheaper, being for the College, I think you are in the Right rather to give what you shall see meet to allow in Gift to the College, in some other Way. . . .[3]

Copley painted a series of large portraits of Harvard's major benefactors, including Thomas Hollis III, Thomas Hancock (H 22, 1766), and Nicholas Boylston (H 90,

1772). All have equally elaborate carved and gilded frames, at the top of which are carved an escutcheon with the family coat of arms.

---

1. Treasurer's Journal, 1755-1773, p. 121. Harvard University Archives (UAI.50.15.56).
2. Allison, "Notes on the Hollis Portraits," p. 5.
3. *Letters and Papers of John Singleton Copley and Henry Pelham, 1739-1776*, p. 75.

87. WILSON, Richard (1714-1782), English

Thomas Hollis V (1720-1774), 1752

Oil on canvas. H. 56.5 x 44.4 cm.
Provenance: Thomas Hollis V; Sir John Dick; Thomas Jenkins; Thomas Brand-Hollis; Rev. John Disney; [Sotheby's]; Mrs. Donald F. Hyde
Lent by Harvard College Library; gift of Mrs. Donald F. Hyde

In the 1750s Thomas Hollis of Lincoln's Inn (Thomas Hollis V) began producing and distributing books, coins, medals, and prints illustrating the history and principles of liberty. He sent these to various institutions in England, France, Italy, Switzerland, Sweden, and America. Financially independent, he devoted his fortune and energies to the cause of liberty.

This "extraordinary one-man propaganda machine," as Bernard Bailyn has called him, sent, in 1758, Milton's works and forty-five other books to the Library of Harvard College. But it was not until after the fire of 1764, which destroyed most of Hollis's previous gifts, along with the scientific apparatus and the rest of the library, that the College received the full benefit of the Englishman's bounty. Hollis advertised in the British newspapers for others to help restore the library of "the dissenting Academy of Harvard in New England," while himself sending £1400 toward restoring Harvard Hall and its contents. Then came the flood (estimated at three to five thousand) of "canonical books," many of them works in the radical Whig tradition.

From this point on, Thomas Hollis focused his attention and benefactions on Massachusetts and Harvard College, in particular. For his "library of liberty," which included works of Locke, Sidney, Marvell, and Neville, Hollis selected the best editions (sometimes his own) and personally supervised their packing and shipping.

Perhaps more important, he became an unofficial agent for Massachusetts in England, championing the colonists' cause. He published and disseminated the writings of such Patriots as Mayhew, Otis, and John Adams, in order that Britain might become aware of their sentiments and grievances. He also tried to keep out of the press any articles or reviews unfavorable to the Americans. Under various pseudonyms, Hollis himself wrote on the colonists' behalf. Samuel Johnson thought of this radical philanthropist as the quintessence of Whiggery and blamed him for the entire Revolution.

While President Holyoke was corresponding with Thomas Hollis V regarding his great-uncle's portrait, he asked for the younger Hollis's portrait, "which will be to us all a most acceptable present." A modest man, Thomas V was as reluctant as Thomas Hollis III had been to forward this gift. After several members of the Harvard Corporation, including Edward Wigglesworth I and Jonathan Mayhew, wrote asking for a portrait, Hollis instead referred them to the principles in the "canonical" books he had donated:

> The effigies which you desire may be seen at this time in the library of Harvard College, feature by feature; though indeed it would require an exact eye, and some time, to cull out, and put those features together, The picture cannot be sent; a print may hereafter, it is possible, when the ideas for it shall have been so settled as to certain matter of more value than the mere likeness of an honest but plain man, an underling in situation and abilities.[1]

Although Hollis's *Memoirs* indicate that he finally sent his "picture" to Harvard, the specific portrait remains unknown. This bust portrait of Hollis came to the College nearly two hundred years after President Holyoke's request. The work is neither signed nor dated, but an inscription on the back of the canvas states that it was painted in 1752 in Rome by R. Wilson. W. G. Constable has attributed this painting to Richard Wilson, an English landscape and portrait painter who was in Italy from 1752 until around 1758.[2]

---

1. W. G. Constable, "A Portrait of Thomas Hollis by Richard Wilson," p. 243. Thomas Hollis to Jonathan Mayhew, 8 May 1766.
2. Hollis, who was a patron of the arts in both Italy and England, commissioned a landscape from Wilson, as well as several paintings of London and Rome by Canaletto (Constable, "Portrait of Hollis," p. 245).

88. CIPRIANI, Giovanni Battista (1727-1785), Italian

Monument to Thomas Hollis, the Younger, 1767

Etching. Plate mark: H. 27.8 x 21.1 cm.
Inscribed, on monument: THOMAE HOLLIS ANGLI / R•ETANT•SS•
LOND•SODALIS / MDCCLXVII; l.l.: I•B•CIPRIANI; l.r.: MDCCLXVII;
below monument: Latin passage from Plutarch's "Life of Brutus"
Fogg Art Museum, Print Department; bequest of Mrs. Frederic T.
Lewis, in memory of Dr. Frederic T. Lewis (M13,864)

On 1 January 1774 Thomas Hollis V died while walking
about his farm in Dorset, to which he had retired. In ac-
cordance with his wishes, his body was buried in the field,
ten feet deep, and immediately plowed over. No trace
was to remain of the burial site. G. B. Cipriani, however,
had earlier produced designs for two proposed Hollis
memorials.[1]

This engraving, *Monument to Thomas Hollis, the
Younger,* may have been one of the prints that Hollis had
told Jonathan Mayhew (see cat. no. 87) he might be sending at a later date.[2]

Monument to Thomas Hollis, the Younger portrays
Hollis in two ways: first, as a Roman, set in a circular
niche on an obelisk decorated with his favorite symbols
and inscriptions and again, as a Georgian gentleman, in
the lower right corner, beneath a branch of oak leaves.
The Latin inscription at the bottom of this print was taken
from Plutarch's "Life of Brutus," one of Hollis's favorite
books.

During Hollis's tour of Italy, he probably saw Roman
republican portrait busts, like the one here, carved in relief on tombstones. Hollis, a collector of antiquities (especially coins and medals), also derived the liberty cap
and assassin's daggers from Roman sources. These symbols, associated with Brutus, who killed the tyrant Caesar,
had long been symbols of freedom. The liberty cap, for
instance, was given to freed Roman slaves to symbolize
their new status.[2] The Fogg Museum owns a Roman coin

of the first century B.C. which depicts Brutus on one side and the liberty cap between daggers on the reverse.

The owl of wisdom seen near the top of the obelisk may have been derived from an Athenian coin, while the inspiration for Britannia was probably the seated Athena, often represented on Hellenistic coins. Britannia sits in her chair of state, on the side of which appears a shield with a Union Jack. She holds a staff with a liberty cap on top in her left hand, and in her right a trident, symbolizing Britain's rule of the sea.[3]

Prints, as well as coins and books, were used by Hollis to promote his political principles. He commissioned prints of the Whig "saints and martyrs," commemorating the figures and events in the history, defense and preservation of liberty.

Although Hollis assisted in the design and general direction, the principal draftsman and engraver of these "liberty prints" — portraits of people such as Sidney, Milton, Mayhew, and Macaulay — was Giovanni Battista Cipriani (see cat. no. 17), who worked for Hollis from at least 1759 until 1770 (the years in which Hollis kept a diary and records Cipriani's frequent visits). Cipriani was also involved in the design of the stamps for the Hollis book-bindings (see cat. no. 97).

---

1. Bond, "Assertor of Liberty," p. 35.
2. On 11 May 1767 the Harvard Corporation thanked Hollis for "two fine Engravings & two etchings del^d to us — the Rev^d Mr. [Andrew] Eliot" (College Records, 2:279, Harvard University Archives. The other engraving they received may have been Hollis's memorial to Rev. Jonathan Mayhew (cat. no. 17), made by Cipriani in the same year as this print.
3. Frank H. Sommer III, "Thomas Hollis and the Arts of Dissent," p. 130.
4. I wish to thank Prof. David Mitten for his help with the classical sources for Hollis's symbols.

89. GREEN, John (1729-1787), English

Thomas Hollis Fencing with Mr. Martin

Oil on canvas. H. 88.9 x 113 cm. Signed and dated, l.l.: J. Green 1746
Lent by the Houghton Library; gift of Arthur A. Houghton, Jr. (*62 z-3)

Thomas Hollis V led a very temperate life. He was a vegetarian and drank only water and tea. He often took cold baths after his early morning exercise, which might consist of riding his horse, walking around London, or fencing in Lombard Street with John Martin.[1]

This scene of Thomas Hollis fencing with the son (left) of his fencing master Mr. Martin (in background) was painted by John Green, an English artist who specialized in mezzotint landscapes.

---

1. Caroline Robbins, "The Strenuous Whig," p. 421.

90A   90B

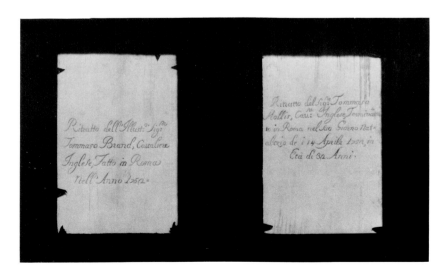

90. POZZI, Andrea (dates unknown), Italian

A. **Thomas Hollis, 1752**

> Ivory. H. 9.5 x 6.1 cm.
> Inscribed, l.c. of obverse: Andrea Pozzi fece dal naturale; of
> reverse: Ritratto del Sig.ᵣₑ Tommaso/Hollis, Cau.ᵣₑ Inglese,
> Termina=/to in Roma nel suo Giorno Nat=/alizio de i 14
> Aprile 1752, in/Età di 32 Anni.

B. **Thomas Brand-Hollis, 1752**

> Ivory. H. 9.5 x 6.1 cm.
> Inscribed, l.c. of obverse: Andrea Pozzi Fecce dal Naturale; of
> reverse: Ritratto dell' Illust.ᵒ Sig.ᵣₑ/Tommaso Brand, Caualiere/
> Inglese, Fatto in Roma/Nell' Anno 1752.
> Lent by the Houghton Library

Thomas Hollis V, "citizen of the world" (as he liked to be known), made two trips to various parts of the continent with his intimate friend and heir, Thomas Brand (honorary LL.D. 1787). In 1748/49 they travelled through France, Switzerland, and northern Italy. A longer journey from 1750 until 1753 took them through northern Germany, Prague, Vienna, Venice, Rome, Florence, Naples, Sicily, and Genoa. They became friends with many artists and scholars residing in those cities.

At Hollis's death in 1774, Brand inherited most of his patron's possessions and land, and in gratitude took his name. He also published Hollis's memoir.

Unlike Thomas Hollis V, Brand-Hollis sought public life and tried to buy his way into the House of Commons. He was subsequently tried and unseated for bribery.

Brand-Hollis continued to correspond with the Boston Whigs and to publish their writings. As a demonstration of his support, he named the great trees on The Hyde, his family estate, for Washington and his fellow revolutionaries.[1]

He also continued the Hollis tradition of generosity to Harvard College. In 1785 he wrote:

> I have this day 4 July, ever to be celebrated and had in
> remembrance, made up a Box of Books various and

mixed, but all I hope will have their use. The larger Number is for the Library of Harvard University, a small Number for the American Academy of Arts and Sciences.[2]

For gifts such as these books and a unique chest microscope (cat. no. 100), Harvard voted in 1787 to award him an LL.D. degree. His name was entered in the Class of 1745, and John Adams, a frequent visitor and correspondent, delivered the diploma to him. Although Brand-Hollis had refused similar honors from British institutions, he accepted this "great honor" from "so illustrious a University."[3]

At his death in 1804, he left the bulk of his estate to Dr. John Disney of London, but bequeathed to Harvard College £100 for Greek and Latin classics for the Library. An admirer of antiquity, Thomas Brand-Hollis had once suggested that the Olympic games be revived in America which, "having acted on Greek principles should have Greek exercises."[4] His death ended a tradition of family beneficence more that a century old.

While in Rome in 1752, Hollis and Brand sat for miniature ivory portraits carved by Andrea Pozzi. The occasion was Hollis's birthday, as indicated by an inscription on the reverse of his "romanized" likeness, to which the Englishman always paid special notice.[5]

Little is known of Pozzi, the Italian ivory carver who crafted these small relief portraits, other than that he apparently was employed for some time by Charles III of Spain.

1. *Sibley's,* 11:553.
2. Samuel Eliot Morison, *Three Centuries of Harvard,* p. 167. Brand-Hollis, a fellow of the Royal Society, had also been elected to the American Academy of Arts and Sciences.
3. *Sibley's,* 11:553.
4. Morison, *Three Centuries,* p. 167.
5. Constable, "Portrait of Hollis," p. 244.

91. Artist Unknown

Hollis Hall, ca. 1800

Ink, watercolor, and tempera on white wove paper. H. 31.8 x 39.7 cm.
Inscribed, l.c.: A Prospect of Hollis — Hall in Cambridge.
Provenance: Arthur Perrin, Brookline, Massachusetts
Lent by Harvard University Archives; gift of Arthur Perrin (HUV 2200.5pf)

By 1761 the College had become overcrowded. More than ninety students lived in private homes in Cambridge, and the Harvard Corporation noted that these students were "less orderly and less well regulated than those within the walls." The Corporation presented a petition for assistance to the Massachusetts General Court, which in 1762 granted Harvard £2,000, and chose a committee to oversee the construction of a new residence hall. The legislature also voted £500 to be paid to Royall Tyler, Esq., "towards purchasing nails, glass, and other materials, in England, for the building of the new College in Cambridge, which . . . Tyler had generously offered to procure for the Province free from any advance or profit."[1]

The building was "well compleated and finished in the best manner" in December 1763 by master builder (and probably designer) Col. Thomas Dawes. It cost £530 over the original appropriation. At a ceremony on 13 January 1764 in Holden Chapel, Gov. Francis Bernard dedicated and named this new dormitory in honor of the Hollis family, whose members were Harvard's most generous benefactors. In a letter to Thomas Hollis V, President Holyoke sent the news that "a very fair building, much more beautiful and commodious than any we had before" had been named for his family. Hollis sent his humble thanks "tho' I have endeavour'd always to be at things rather than appearances, for the active part which You have taken in the nomination of the new building at Your college, and bestowing on it the name of *Hollis Hall.*"[2]

The brick structure (103 feet long by 43 feet wide) con-

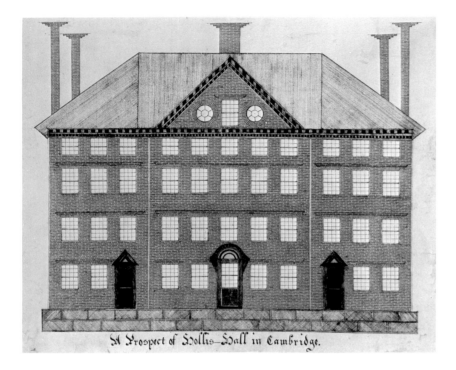

A Prospect of Hollis-Hall in Cambridge.

tained thirty-two rooms, arranged in the medieval chamber-and-study fashion. The rooms and cellar bins (where students kept their fuel, liquor, and other supplies) were rented at a rate which produced £100 annually.[3]

During the time that Washington's soldiers used Hollis Hall as barracks it was damaged, as were the other Harvard buildings. Harvard petitioned for reimbursement of such items as thirty-one brass knob locks, sixty-three study locks, and ninety-four rolls of paper.

This simple, yet elegant, watercolor of Hollis Hall was probably executed ca. 1800 by a Harvard student.

1. H. A. Clas and F. O. Vaille, *The Harvard Book,* 1:64.
2. Hamilton Vaughan Bail, *Views of Harvard,* pp. 53-54.
3. Ten pounds was to go toward repair of the building, while the rest supported the tutors and purchased books (Clas and Vaille, *Harvard Book,* 1:65).

92. Jebb, Samuel, editor (1694?-1772)

Bibliotheca literaria, being a collection of inscriptions, medals, dissertations . . .

London: W. and J. Innys, 1722-24. H. 22.7 cm.
Lent by the Houghton Library; gift of Thomas Hollis (x27.20.76)

Thomas Hollis V had written to Edmund Quincy on 1 October 1766, explaining his gifts to Harvard:

> I confess to bear affection towards the people of North America, those of Massachusetts and Boston, in particular, believing them to be a good and brave people; long may they continue such! and the spirit of luxury now consuming us to the very marrow here at home, keep out from them! One likeliest mean to that end will be, to watch well over their youth, by bestowing on them a reasonable, manly education; and selecting thereto the wisest, ablest, most accomplished of men, that art and wealth can obtain; for nations rise and fall by individuals, not numbers, as I think all history proveth. With ideas of this kind have I worked for the public library at Cambridge, in New England, neither caring too exactly to remember how the late best library in all America was lost there, nor sparing towards its expense, labor, and time.[1]

In this book, given to Harvard in 1767, he further spelled out his reasons, writing, as he often did, in the third person:

> In the beginning, He sent Books on Government, beside stray Books, to Harvard College; for, if Government goeth right, ALL goeth right. Then, He sent Grammars, Dictionaries, of Root and other Languages, with critical Authors; in hope of forming first rate Scholars, the NOBLEST of all Men! Now, he dribblets out the like. And thinks, to take his leave.

In 1722 Samuel Jebb, a physician, began publishing this classical periodical. The ten issues bound together in this volume date 1722-24.

---

1. Quincy, *History of Harvard*, 2:146-47.

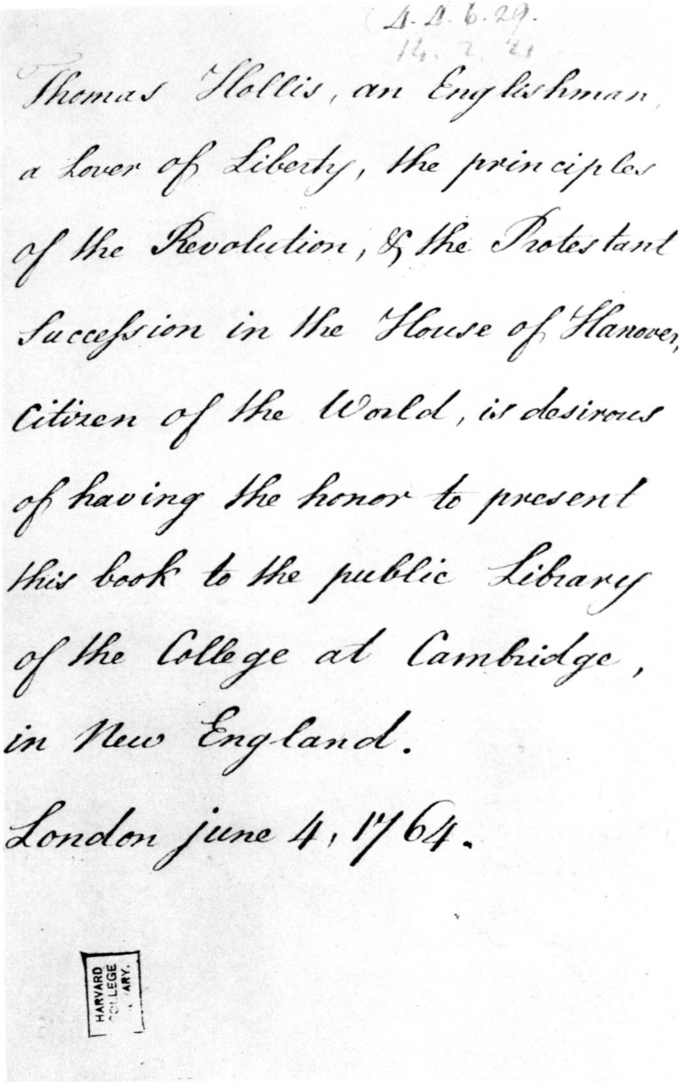

A.A.6.29.
14.2.2

Thomas Hollis, an Englishman, a lover of Liberty, the principles of the Revolution, & the Protestant Succession in the House of Hanover, Citizen of the World, is desirous of having the honor to present this book to the public Library of the College at Cambridge, in New England.

London june 4, 1764.

93. Locke, John (1632-1704)

Two Treatises of Government . . .

London: A. Millar, 1764. 6th edition. H. 20 cm.
Lent by the Houghton Library; gift of Thomas Hollis (x27.20.38)

To educate the "ingenuous Youth of Harvard College," Hollis edited and published several "canonical" works by authors whom he felt illustrated the principles of liberty. His sixth edition of John Locke's *Two Treatises of Government*, which was the best available edition in English until 1960 was one of them.[1] In 1764 Thomas Hollis, "an Englishman, a Lover of Liberty, the principles of the Revolution, of the Protestant Succession in the House of Hanover, Citizen of the World. . . ." inscribed and presented this copy to Harvard College.

---

1. Charles W. Akers, *Called Unto Liberty*, p. xii.

94. Sidney, Algernon (1622-1683)

Discourses Concerning Government

London: A. Millar, 1751. 3rd edition. H. 37.5 cm.
Lent by the Houghton Library; bequest of James Walker, D.D., LL.D., late president of Harvard College (x27.20.4)

Sidney's *Discourses Concerning Government*, written in 1698, was republished in 1751 by Andrew Millar.[1] Hollis sent the book to his friends in America because he considered Sidney, "the martyr of civil liberty," to be one of the greatest English political theorists.[2]

This is one of four known volumes containing six prints of a portrait of Algernon Sidney at age forty-one. A long inscription, written by Hollis on the flyleaf, tells the story of the prints. George Vertue made a drawing of this portrait after a painting, attributed to the Belgian artist Justus van Egmont (ca. 1601-1674), owned by the Sidney family. Hollis goes on to relate how "a gentleman purchased the Drawing; and that the Memory of so excellent a Person might be still better preserved and extended, He caused a print to be made from it. . . ."[3] John Baptist Jackson (1701-ca. 1780) of Battersea was commissioned to make this woodcut after Vertue's drawing.[4]

In 1755 Hollis anonymously sent the Sidney portrait and book to the colonies. Jasper Maudit, a friend of Hollis's and later a colonial agent, wrote to Jonathan Mayhew on 28 February 1755:

> At the request of a Gentleman lately returned from his travells, & has brought home a confirm'd Sence of English liberty, I have put on board . . . a box, containing some prints of that great statesman Algernon Sidney, also a set for Hayward College, & a Sidney bound, as a present for your self. Some of these prints are sent to Connecticut & the other provinces which may have their use. . . .[5]

This was but one of several gifts that Hollis made in an effort to promote Sidney's philosophy in New England. In 1760/61 he commissioned Cipriani to etch and engrave a portrait of Sidney, which was distributed to the colonies; and in 1763 a new *Discourses Concerning Government* was issued and sent to Harvard College.

1. Millar (1707-1768) also reprinted Jonathan Mayhew's writings.

2. Sommer, "Thomas Hollis and the Arts of Dissent," p. 132.

3. Quoted from flyleaf of this volume.

4. Jackson had been trained in both France and Italy, and was active as a designer of wallpaper. He was patronized by Thomas Hollis V and Thomas Brand-Hollis (Sommer, p. 133).

95. Milton, John (1608-1674)

The Works . . .

London: A. Millar, 1753. H. 29 cm.
Lent by the Houghton Library; gift of Thomas Hollis (x27.20.10, v.2)

Hollis's favorite seventeenth-century radical was the "MATCHLESS John Milton."[1] This book arrived as part of Hollis's earliest donation to Harvard in 1764. Included in the volume is Milton's "History of Britain."

The front and rear covers are elaborately tooled in gold on green leather. Britannia is shown seated on a shield, holding a staff in her left hand and an olive branch in her right. A star shines over her, while "O FAIR BRITANNIA HAIL!" is stamped below. An acorn wreath encloses this design.

---

1. Hollis named one of his farms Milton. Others were called Harvard, Liberty, and Sidney (Bond, "Assertor of Liberty," p. 33).

96. Cortonese, Ridolfina Venuti (1705-1763)

D'Escrizone Topografica delle Antichità di Roma. Parte Prima

Rome: Battista Bernabò, 1763. H. 27 cm.

Lent by the Houghton Library, Department of Printing and Graphic Arts; from the collection of Philip Hofer, Class of 1921 (Typ 725.63.868[A])

Hollis sent books not only on government, but also on economics, aesthetics, and travel. This volume, a topographical description of ancient Rome, was sold at the estate of John Disney (Thomas Brand-Hollis's heir) at Sotheby's in March 1871. It includes scenes of Rome engraved by Giovanni Battista Piranesi (1720-1778).

Symbolic devices — Britannia with liberty cap and staff, crowned by a star and flanked by palm and olive branches — stamped in gold into the red morocco leather, are placed upright on the front cover, but are upside down on the rear cover. This was Hollis's way of indicating the rise and fall of Rome.[1] Symbols also appear on the binding (rooster, palm branch, star, liberty cap, olive branch, and owl), as well as on the flyleaf, where smoke prints made from the Britannia and Apollo's lyre stamps may be found.

Hollis not only subscribed to the work of the Abbé Ridolfina Venuti, the author of this book, but donated a great deal of financial aid to his projects.[2]

1. Hollis also sometimes inverted the stamps to indicate his disapproval of a work or its author.
2. Robbins, "The Strenuous Whig," p. 411.

97. CIPRIANI, Giovanni Battista (1727-1785)

Designs for Nineteen Binding Tools, ca. 1764

Ink on cream antique laid paper
   A. H. 18.9 x 9.2 cm.   B. H. 19.6 x 12.2 cm.
Lent by the Houghton Library, Department of Printing and Graphic Arts; gift of Arthur A. Houghton, Jr. (ms Typ 576[15])

In 1764 the same year that a fire destroyed Harvard's library, another fire at Thomas Hollis's bookbinder in London destroyed the tools for Hollis's symbolic devices. Giovanni Battista Cipriani was commissioned to design new emblems, derived from ancient Greek and Roman coins and medals collected by Hollis, to be representative of both freedom and learning.[1] Thomas Pingo, an engraver of medals, used Cipriani's drawings to make seventeen new brass dies for stamping these symbols in gold on the rich red morocco book bindings.

The sumptuous bindings were meant to seize the student's attention:

> The Bindings of Books are little regarded by me for my own library; but by long experience I have found it necessary to attend to them for other libraries; having thereby drawn notice, with preservation, on many excellent books, or curious, which it is probable, would else have passed unheeded and neglected.[2]

Once the student's attention was drawn to the books, the classical symbols were to describe the nature of the work. But Caroline Robbins believes that even an eighteenth-century student who had been educated in the classics might not have fully understood Hollis's complex code.[3] Many of the symbols seen here are attributes of the deities of the classical world: the cornucopia of Demeter; the club of Hercules; the trident of Neptune; the caduceus of Hermes; the lyre of Apollo; the owl of Athena.

1. Bond, "Assertor of Liberty," p. 35.
2. Robbins, "The Strenuous Whig," p. 426.
3. *Ibid.,* p. 425.
4. Once again, Prof. David Mitten has helped with the interpretation of the classical symbols.

98. COPLEY, John Singleton (1738-1815), American

John Winthrop (1714-1779), Hollis Professor of Mathematics and Natural Philosophy, 1773

Oil on canvas. H. 127.5 x 102.5 cm.
Harvard University Portrait Collection; gift of the executors of the estate of John Winthrop of Rhode Island, grandson of Professor Winthrop, to Harvard College, in 1894 (H 113)

A prize student, John Winthrop (A.B. 1732; LL.D. 1773) entered Harvard at age thirteen. At the age of twenty-four, he was appointed second Hollis Professor of Mathematics and Natural Philosophy.

Winthrop's Philosophy Chamber, stocked with the scientific apparatus donated by the Hollis family, Thomas Hancock, James Bowdoin, Andrew Oliver, Jr., and others, became the colonial center for the study of astronomy and physics. Professor Winthrop used these instruments to give demonstrations of Newtonian principles. His observations and studies pioneered the study of science in eighteenth-century America. He conducted the first practical demonstrations and experiments in electricity and magnetism, analyzed earthquakes as well as sunspots and solar eclipses, and recorded the passage of Halley's comet through New England skies. He also studied the transit of Mercury and led the first American astronomical expedition, in 1761, to Newfoundland, to observe the transit of Venus.[1]

For these and other contributions to science, John Winthrop was elected to the Royal Society in 1766, probably at the behest of his friend and fellow scientist, Benjamin Franklin. Winthrop and his students published some of their discoveries and observations in the Society's journal, *Philosophical Transactions*.

An excellent and popular teacher, he was also an active fellow of the Harvard Corporation, to which he was named in 1765. Winthrop became acting president of the College following Holyoke's death in 1768, and again in

1773/74. Although he was elected president in 1774, he refused the office, preferring his teaching and research to the administrative duties. In 1773 he was awarded an LL.D., the first time that Harvard had ever bestowed that honor.

The eminent scientist became involved in politics through the influence of such former students as Sam Adams, "Jemmy" Otis, and John Hancock. He was such a trusted Patriot that he was one of the five men to whom Franklin sent copies of the Hutchinson-Oliver Letters. He served in the Provincial Congress and the Council, where he was a member of a committee to draw up a list of the Boston Tories and their offenses.

Winthrop's death in 1779 was mourned throughout Massachusetts. Three funeral sermons and several obituaries were published, and both Mercy Otis Warren (cat. no. 9) and Andrew Oliver, Jr. (cat. no. 37) wrote poems in his honor. Oliver's poem follows:

> Ye Sons of Harvard! Who, by Winthrop taught,
> Can travel round each planetary sphere;
> And, wing'd with his rapidity of thought,
> Trace all the movements of the rolling year;
> Drop on his urn the tribute of a tear.[2]

1. *Sibley's,* 9:253.
2. *Ibid.,* p. 263.

99. BIRD, John (1709-1776), English

Meridian Telescope and Equal Altitudes Instrument, 1768

Brass (fitted to iron shaft and mahogany stand). Barrel: L. 99 cm.; DIAM. 4 cm.
Inscribed, on barrel: J. BIRD, LONDON.
Lent by the Collection of Historical Scientific Instruments; gift of Thomas Hollis of Lincoln's Inn, 1767 (No. 58)

In 1767 Thomas Hollis V gave £200 to Harvard for the purpose of replacing some of the scientific or "philo-

sophical" apparatus destroyed in the 1764 fire. The Corporation advised that the money be used to purchase, among other items, a combined meridian telescope and equal altitudes instrument.

Professor Winthrop asked his friend Benjamin Franklin to assist in obtaining the instruments from craftsmen in London, and Franklin placed orders with James Short, Benjamin Martin, and John Bird. Franklin reported in 1768 that Bird's work was slow, since the craftsman insisted on doing all the work himself. Bird, who was famous for this type of instrument, was especially in demand in the late 1760s, making scientific instruments for customers in England, Russia, and France who wanted to observe the 1769 transit of Venus. The instrument Franklin had ordered finally arrived safely in Cambridge for use by Professor Winthrop and his students.

This meridian telescope and equal altitudes instrument has been traditionally assumed to be the one made by Bird, and a recent cleaning has verified the attribution by revealing the inscription: J. BIRD, LONDON.

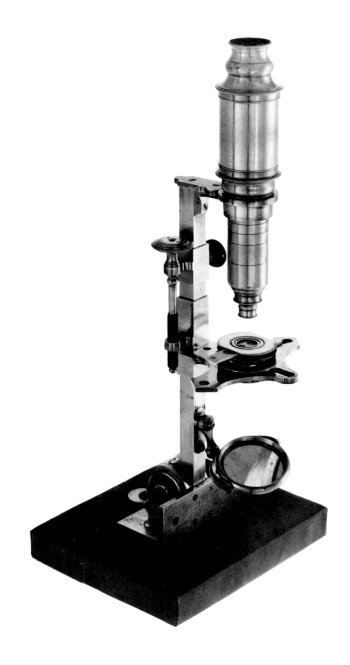

100. NAIRNE, Edward (1726-1806), English

Chest Microscope, 1792

Brass. Stand: H. 24.8 cm.; barrel: L. 18.5 cm.
Inscribed, on stage of microscope: NAIRNE Invt. et Fecit LONDON
Lent by the Collection of Historical Scientific Instruments; gift of
  Thomas Brand-Hollis, 1792 (No. 42)

Thomas Brand-Hollis presented this compound microscope to Harvard College in 1792. This instrument, invented by Edward Nairne, was fastened to a chest into which it could be folded for storage. The chest has since been lost.

Bibliography

Adair, Douglass and Schutz, John A., eds. *Peter Oliver's Origins of the American Rebellion: A Tory View*. Stanford, Calif.: Stanford University Press, 1961.

Adams, Charles Francis, ed. *Familiar Letters of John Adams and His Wife Abigail Adams, During the Revolution*. Cambridge, Mass.: The Riverside Press, 1876.

Akers, Charles W. *Called Unto Liberty: A Life of Jonathan Mayhew 1720-1766*. Cambridge: Harvard University Press, 1964.

Allen, Charles Dexter. *American Book-Plates*. London: George Bell & Sons, 1895.

Allison, Anne. "Notes on the Hollis Portraits." Mimeographed. Cambridge: Harvard University Archives, 1937.

Ambler, Louise Todd. *Benjamin Franklin: A Perspective*. Cambridge: Fogg Art Museum, Harvard University, 1975.

Anthony, Katharine. *First Lady of the Revolution: The Life of Mercy Otis Warren*. Garden City, New York: Doubleday & Co., Inc., 1958.

Bail, Hamilton Vaughan. *Views of Harvard: A Pictorial Record to 1860*. Cambridge: Harvard University Press, 1949.

Bailyn, Bernard. "Butterfield's Adams: Notes for a Sketch." *William and Mary Quarterly* 3rd series. 19 (April 1962):238-256.

————. *The Ideological Origins of the American Revolution*. Cambridge: Harvard University Press, 1967.

————. *The Ordeal of Thomas Hutchinson*. Cambridge: Harvard University Press, 1974.

————. "Religion and Revolution: Three Biographical Studies." *Perspectives in American History* 4(1970):85-169.

Batchelder, Samuel. *Bits of Harvard History*. Cambridge: Harvard University Press, 1924.

————. "Burgoyne and His Officers in Cambridge, 1777-1778." *Publications of the Cambridge Historical Society* 13(1918):17-80.

————. "Col. Henry Vassall and His Wife Penelope Vassall with Some Account of His Slaves." *Publications of the Cambridge Historical Society* 10(1917):5-85.

Bond, William. "Assertor of Liberty, Citizen of the World." *Harvard Magazine* 76(March 1974):33-35.

Boston Museum of Fine Arts. *American Paintings in the Museum of Fine Arts, Boston*. Boston: Distributed by the New York Graphic Society, Greenwich, Conn., 1969.

Bowditch, Harold. "Early Water-Color Paintings of New England Coats of Arms." *Publications of the Colonial Society of Massachusetts* 35(1942-46):172-210.

Bowen, Catherine Drinker. *The Most Dangerous Man in America: Scenes from the Life of Benjamin Franklin*. Boston: Little, Brown, & Co., 1974.

Brennan, Ellen. "James Otis: Recreant and Patriot." *New England Quarterly* 12(December 1939):691-725.

Bridenbaugh, Carl. *Peter Harrison: First American Architect*. Chapel Hill, N.C.: University of North Carolina Press, 1949.

Brigham, Clarence S. *Paul Revere's Engravings*. Rev. ed. New York: Atheneum, 1969.

Brown, John Perkins. "Christ Church, Cambridge." *Publications of the Cambridge Historical Society* 23(1934-35):17-23.

Brown, Percy W. "The Sojourn of Harvard College in Concord." *Harvard Graduates' Magazine* 27(1892):497-509.

Buck, J. D. *Old Plate: Its Makers and Marks*. New and enlarged edition. New York: The Gorham Manufacturing Co., 1903.

Buhler, Kathryn C. *American Silver, 1655-1825, in the Museum of Fine Arts, Boston*. 2 vols. Boston: Museum of Fine Arts, 1972.

Burroughs, Alan. *John Greenwood in America 1745-1752.* Andover, Mass.: Addison Gallery of American Art, 1943.

_____. "Paintings by Nathaniel Smibert." *Art in America* 31(April 1943):88-97.

Butterfield, Lyman H. et al., eds. *Diary and Autobiography of John Adams.* 4 vols. Cambridge: Belknap Press of Harvard University Press, 1961.

Clas, H. A. and Vaille, F. O. *The Harvard Book: A Series of Historical, Biographical, and Descriptive Sketches by Various Authors.* 2 vols. Cambridge, Mass.: Welch, Bigelow, & Co., 1875.

Cohen, I. Bernard. *Some Early Tools of American Science.* Cambridge: Harvard University Press, 1950.

Constable, W. G. "A Portrait of Thomas Hollis by Richard Wilson." *Harvard Library Bulletin* 5(Spring 1951):242-46.

Dana, Henry Wadsworth Longfellow. "The Longfellow House." *Old-Time New England* 38(April 1948):81-96.

Day, Gardiner M. *Biography of a Church.* Cambridge, Mass.: Privately printed at the Riverside Press, 1951.

The Dictionary of American Biography. Edited by Allen Johnson and Dumas Malone. New York: Charles Scribner's Sons, 1931.

The Dictionary of National Biography. Edited by Sir Leslie Stephen and Sir Sidney Lee. London: Oxford University Press, 1949-50.

Dow, George Francis. *The Arts and Crafts of New England 1704-1775.* Topsfield, Mass.: The Wayside Press, 1927.

Drake, Francis S., ed. *Tea Leaves: Being a Collection of Letters and Documents Relating to the Shipment of Tea to the American Colonies in the Year 1773, By the East India Tea Company.* Boston: A. O. Crane, 1884.

Dresser, Louisa. "Edward Savage, Painter 1761-1817." *Art in America* 40(Autumn 1952):157-212.

Elkins, Kimball C. "Honorary Degrees at Harvard." *Harvard Library Bulletin* 12(Autumn 1958):326-353.

Elton, Oliver. "Lieutenant Governor Thomas Oliver, 1734-1815." *Publications of the Colonial Society of Massachusetts* 28(1930-33): 37-66.

Flynt, Henry N. and Fales, Martha Gandy. *The Heritage Foundation Collection of Silver with Biographical Sketches of New England Silversmiths, 1625-1825.* Deerfield, Mass.: Heritage Foundation, 1968.

Foote, Henry Wilder. "Benjamin Blyth of Salem: Eighteenth-Century Artist." *Proceedings of the Massachusetts Historical Society* 71 (1953-57):64-107.

_____. *John Smibert, Painter.* Cambridge: Harvard University Press, 1950.

_____. *Robert Feke: Colonial Portrait Painter.* Cambridge: Harvard University Press, 1930.

Ford, Worthington Chauncy. "Mrs. Warren's 'The Group.'" *Proceedings of the Massachusetts Historical Society* 62(1928-29):15-22.

Franklin, Benjamin. "Tract Relating to the Affair of Hutchinson's Letters." In *The Writings of Benjamin Franklin*, edited by Albert Henry Smyth, 6:258-289. New York: The MacMillan Co., 1907.

Fraser, Esther Stevens. "The John Hicks House." *Publications of the Cambridge Historical Society* 20(1927-29):110-124.

Freiberg, Malcolm. "Thomas Hutchinson: The First Fifty Years (1711-1761)." *William and Mary Quarterly* 3rd series. 15(January 1958):35-55.

French, Hollis. *Jacob Hurd and His Sons Nathaniel and Benjamin, Silversmiths, 1702-1781.* Cambridge, Mass.: Riverside Press, 1939.

Garrett, Wendell D. *Apthorp House 1760-1960.* Cambridge: Harvard University Press, 1960.

"Gawen and Mather Brown." *Proceedings of the Massachusetts Historical Society* 47(March-April 1914):289-293.

Gozzaldi, Mary Isabella. "Elmwood and Its Owners." *Publications of the Cambridge Historical Society* 15(1921):41-45.

Groce, Henry C. and Wallace, David J. *The New-York Historical Society's Dictionary of Artists in America, 1564-1860.* New Haven: Yale University Press, 1957.

Hall, B. H. *A Collection of College Words and Customs.* Rev. and enlarged edition. New York: M. Doolady, 1859.

Huntsinger, Laura M. *Harvard Portraits: A Catalogue . . .* Edited by Alan Burroughs. Cambridge: Harvard University Press, 1936.

Hutcheson, Maud Macdonald. "Mercy Warren, 1728-1814." *William and Mary Quarterly* 3rd series. 10(July 1953):378-402.

James, Edward T., ed. *Notable American Women 1607-1950*, vol. 1 (A-F). Cambridge: Belknap Press of Harvard University Press, 1971.

Jones, E. Alfred. *The Loyalists of Massachusetts: Their Memorials, Petitions, and Claims.* London: The Saint Catherine Press, 1930.

_____. *The Old Silver of American Churches.* Privately printed for the National Society of the Colonial Dames of America, at the Arden Press, Letchworth, England, 1913.

Lane, William C. "The Building of Massachusetts Hall, 1717-1720." *Publications of the Colonial Society of Massachusetts* 24(April 1920):81-110.

————. "Early Views of Harvard College." *Harvard Graduates' Magazine* 12(March 1904):349-358.

Letters and Papers of John Singleton Copley and Henry Pelham, 1739-1776. Collections, no. 71. Boston: Massachusetts Historical Society, 1914.

Lillie, Rupert Ballou. *Cambridge in 1775.* Salem, Mass.: Newcomb & Gauss Co., 1949.

Middlesex County (Mass.) Probate Records.

Miller, Lillian. *In the Minds and Hearts of the People: Prologue to the American Revolution: 1760-1775.* Greenwich, Conn.: New York Graphic Society, 1974.

Mooz, R. Peter. "Colonial Art." In *The Genius of American Painting,* edited by John Wilmerding, pp. 26-78. London: Weidenfeld & Nicolson, 1973.

Morgan, John H. and Fielding, Mantle. *Life Portraits of George Washington and their Replicas.* Philadelphia: Printed for the subscribers, 1931.

Morison, Samuel Eliot. *Three Centuries of Harvard, 1636-1936.* Cambridge: Harvard University Press, 1936.

Oliver, Andrew, comp. *Faces of a Family,* Boston: Privately printed, 1960.

————. "Peter Pelham (c. 1697-1751) Sometime Printmaker of Boston." In *Boston Prints and Printmakers 1670-1775,* edited by Walter Muir Whitehill and Sinclair Hitchings, pp. 133-73. Boston: Colonial Society of Massachusetts, 1973.

————. *Portraits of John and Abigail Adams.* Cambridge: Belknap Press of the Harvard University Press, 1967.

Paige, Lucius R. *History of Cambridge, Massachusetts, 1630-1877.* 2 vols. Cambridge, Mass.: The Riverside Press, 1877.

Park, Lawrence. *Gilbert Stuart.* 4 vols. New York: William Edwin Rudge, 1926.

————. "Joseph Blackburn: Portrait Painter." *Proceedings of the American Antiquarian Society* n.s. 32(1922):270-329.

Parker, Barbara N. and Wheeler, Anne B. *John Singleton Copley, American Portraits in Oil, Pastel, and Miniature.* Boston: Museum of Fine Arts, 1938.

Prown, Jules David. *John Singleton Copley.* 2 vols. Cambridge: Harvard University Press, 1966.

Quincy, Josiah. *The History of Harvard University.* 2 vols. Cambridge, Mass.: John Owen, 1840.

Reed, Christopher. "New England Education's First Maecenas." *Harvard Magazine* 76(October 1973):31-32.

Riley, Stephen T. "John Smibert and The Business of Portrait Painting." In *American Painting to 1776: A Reappraisal,* edited by Ian M. G. Quimby, pp. 159-180. Charlottesville, Va.: The University Press of Virginia, 1971.

Robbins, Caroline. "The Strenuous Whig: Thomas Hollis of Lincoln's Inn." *William and Mary Quarterly* 3rd series. 7(July 1950): 406-453.

Sanborn, Franklin B. "Samuel Langdon." *Proceedings of the Massachusetts Historical Society* 2nd series. 18(1903-04):192-232.

Sellers, Charles Coleman. *Benjamin Franklin in Portraiture.* New Haven: Yale University Press, 1962.

————. "Mezzotint Prototypes of Colonial Portraiture: A Summary Based on the Research of Waldron Phoenix Belknap, Jr.," *Art Quarterly* 20(Winter 1957):407-468.

Sibley's Harvard Graduates: Biographical Sketches of Those Who Attended Harvard College . . . 16 vols. Boston: Massachusetts Historical Society, 1873-19——.

Smibert, John. *The Notebook of John Smibert.* With Essays by Sir David Evans, John Kerslake and Andrew Oliver. And with Notes Relating to Smibert's American Portraits by Andrew Oliver. Boston: Massachusetts Historical Society, 1969.

Smith, John Chaloner. *British Mezzotinto Portraits.* 4 vols. London: Henry Sotheran & Co., 1883.

Sommer, Frank H., III. "Thomas Hollis and the Arts of Dissent." In *Prints in and of America to 1850,* edited by John D. Morse, pp. 111-159. Charlottesville, Va.: The University Press of Virginia, 1970.

Stark, James H. *The Loyalists of Massachusetts.* 1910. Reprint. Clifton, N.J.: Augustus M. Kelley, 1972.

Stauffer, David McNeely. *American Engravers Upon Copper and Steel.* 2 vols. New York: The Grolier Club, 1907.

Stephens, Frederic G. and Hawkins, Edward. *Catalogue of Prints and Drawings in The British Museum.* Division I, Political and Personal Satires, vol. 4 1761-1770. London: Printed by the Order of the Trustees (Chiswick Press), 1883.

Swan, Mabel M. "Furniture of the Boston Tories." *Antiques* 41 (March 1942):186-89.

Ward, George Atkinson. *Journal & Letters of Samuel Curwen.* New York: C. S. Francis & Co., 1842.

Warren, Charles. *History of the Harvard Law School and of Early Legal Conditions in America.* 3 vols. New York: Lewis Publishing Co., 1908.

Warren, Mercy Otis. *History of the Rise, Progress, and Termination of the American Revolution.* 3 vols. Boston: Manning and Loring, 1804.

Warren-Adams Letters. Collections, nos. 72 and 73. Boston: Massachusetts Historical Society, 1917 and 1925.

Waters, John J., Jr. *The Otis Family in Provincial and Revolutionary Massachusetts.* Chapel Hill, N.C.: University of North Carolina Press, 1968.

Watkins, Walter Kendall. "John Coles, Heraldry Painter." *Old-Time New England* 21(January 1931):129-142.

Wheatland, David P. *The Apparatus of Science at Harvard, 1765-1800.* Cambridge: Harvard University Press, 1968.

Whitehill, Walter Muir; Fairbanks, Jonathan; and Cooper, Wendy. *Paul Revere's Boston, 1735-1818.* Boston: Museum of Fine Arts, Boston, 1975.

Victoria and Albert Museum. *Catalogue of Water Colour Paintings by British Artists and Foreigners Working in Britain.* Rev. ed. London: Printed Under the Authority of the Board of Education, 1927.

Vincent, Gilbert. "The Bombé Furniture of Boston." In *Boston Furniture of the Eighteenth Century,* edited by Walter Muir Whitehill, Brock Jobe and Jonathan Fairbanks. Boston: Colonial Society of Massachusetts, 1974.

Index

Photography Credits

Paul Birnbaum: 15B, 43, 64, 68, 72, 78. Richard Cheek: 13, 30, 39, 42. George M. Cushing: 4, 62. Daniel Farber: 5, 11. Frick Art Reference Library: 23, 31, 37, 38. Jock Gill and Jon Halberstadt: 80. Helga Photo Studio: 21. Michael Nedzweski: 10, 14, 15A, 16, 18, 19, 22, 24, 25, 26, 32, 33, 35, 40, 41, 46, 47, 48, 49, 50, 52, 53, 57, 61, 63 A & B, 65, 66, 67 A & B, 69, 71, 75, 77, 90 A & B, 91, 92, 97, 99. Herbert P. Vose: 1.